MW01223324

בס"ד

A Chassid,
A Businessman

The Story of
Zalman Deitsch

Dovid Zaklikowski

A Chassid, A Businessman © 2020 Deitsch Family 518

www.LubavitchArchives.com
LubavitchArchives@gmail.com

ISBN 978-1-944875-13-8

Design by Hasidic Archives Studios

Cover by Spotlight Design

Printed in Bulgaria

Please send comments to Book.ZalmanDeitsch@gmail.com

To our dear mother
Mrs. Cyrel Deitsch

Index

[IV]
The Businessman

[V]
The Family Man

[Part VI]
Merging Two Worlds

[Part VII]
An Open Hand

[Part VIII]
Never Forgotten

Appendixes

Introduction

A SUDDEN RESPONSIBILITY

Our father was a twenty-two-year-old *bochur* engaged to be married when he suddenly lost his father. The burden of supporting the family immediately fell on his shoulders.

Our father wanted to go on *shlichus*. However, in the most vital *yechidus* of his life, the Rebbe instructed him to go into his father's business.

This yechidus took place during our father's engagement, with his entire family present. His mother, Mirel, at the time a widow with little children, in despair and grieving over the death of her husband, blurted out, "He is a *batlan*!" She meant that our father's head was until now in the holy books of the Torah, and he knew nothing of business dealings. How could he provide for his mother, four siblings, and a new wife?

The Rebbe gave his assurance and blessing, saying, "He will yet learn." Toward the end of the yechidus, the Rebbe advised our grandmother to have *emunah* and *bitachon,* and it will be *b'yeser s'eos u'byser oz*—have faith and trust in Hashem, and he will have success with much vigor.

Balancing Different Worlds

Fifty years later, it is with humility and gratitude that we, the family of Zalman Deitsch, *alav hashalom,* present this book about our dear father: *A Chassid, A Businessman.*

Despite our grandmother's concern, our father went on to become successful in business. He was highly active in the textile industry, flying throughout the U.S., then internationally to Africa, and eventually opening up a business in Honduras, the Dominican Republic in South America and Mexico City. The business world never distracted our father from his identity as a Chassid. He had a gift for balancing business with his love for the Rebbe's *mivtzoim* and Torah (*sichos, maamarim*). Throughout his life, he remained a Chassid.

As children, we barely knew what he did for a living; we almost never went to "the *platz*," as he called his place of business, to see what he did. Whenever we asked him about his day, he would respond with questions about ours. Even as children we wondered: How is it possible for anyone to be a successful businessman without ever carrying his business achievements and concerns home from the office?

Our underlying question was: How was he able to balance two worlds, each demanding in a different way?

Work, Family, and Community

To be successful in business, you must be totally engaged in work. You must deal with many factors you cannot predict or control. How does a businessperson just turn off the world according to the demands of the Jewish calendar? What do you do if you have to return calls or resolve a problem at the warehouse when at the same time you want to prepare for *yom tov*? How do you prioritize? Are you a Chassid or a businessman?

Raising a family also demands time. The Rebbe encouraged young couples to have many children. Our parents took this to heart, and we are, *kein ayin hara*, a big bunch. Our father was devoted to our mother, *zol gezunt zein*, and loved to spend time with his kids, talking to us and learning with us.

Then there are the demands of our community: Our father also sat on committees of different mivtzos and *mosdos* of the Rebbe, as well as found time for personal learning. He also spent time with countless individuals who sought his counsel.

The challenge many of us face today is that we are pulled in too many directions. We are wired to our businesses during times we should be focused on the needs of our spouses or children. When attending a *shiur*, we may easily be distracted by financial dealings or personal problems. How was our father able to be so fully attentive, in both mind and heart, in every single area of human activity? How did he compartmentalize his life so successfully?

You will find the answers in the pages of this book.

An Ultimate Purpose

We have worked diligently to select inspirational stories to portray our father's life.

Our father was a humble man who didn't see his success as his own.

Our father was a man who embraced life to the fullest, through dark times and bright ones, through laughter and tears.

Our father was a man who utilized every moment of his day to its maximum potential.

He bore the heartache of losing some of his closest relatives, who passed away at young ages. He saw his business burned to the ground one year, and suffered a great flood the next. Yet he endured. Throughout the years, he managed to conduct his business affairs, here and in other countries, with the blessings of the Rebbe.

Most important of all, our father never lost sight of his life's purpose. Work was that, and nothing more; he never let it get to his head. To him, his *tafkid* in life was to give the Rebbe *nachas* (as he would constantly write in his *pan*), to give as much *tzedakah* as he could, and then give more.

Expressions of Gratitude

We would like to take this opportunity to say a heartfelt thank you to the over fifty individuals who shared their memories and stories for this book—first for the original Hebrew edition (*Va'yehi Ish Matzliach*), and now for this new and revised English translation.

This book would never have been published without the input and blessings of our dear mother, Mrs. Cyrel Deitsch, who allowed us to share the life story of a very private man for the purpose of providing lessons that we can all learn from. *Thank you for permitting us to share it with the public.*

A special thanks also goes to our dear uncle Avraham Moshe Deitsch for his insights and suggestions, which improved the text immeasurably.

Thank you to our brother Nechemia, who, together with his wife D'vory, spearheaded this project. They made sure that every detail, first in the Hebrew edition and now in the English, was handled in a precise and correct manner.

We also thank our dear brothers Shaya and Mendy for their

tireless devotion to seeing this project through to the end; our brothers Chessy and Sruli for collecting all of the pictures for publication; and our sisters Toby, Altie, Hindy, Rivki, and Rochel for their deep insights, shared memories, and sensitivity as this book was formulated.

Furthermore, this book would not have been possible without the constant encouragement and support of our brothers- and sisters-in-law.

We are forever indebted to Menachem Z. and his sister Tammy Holtzman for conducting the interviews and writing the original Hebrew edition.

This rewritten and reworked English edition would never have happened without the tireless efforts of Dovid Zaklikowski, Sarah Ogince, Yitzchok Cohen, Miriam Palace, and the rest of the staff at Hasidic Archives. To them we say a huge *yasher koach*.

Thanks to Jewish Educational Media for giving us permission to use pictures for this book and for all the work they do on behalf of the Rebbe and the Lubavitch community. Thanks to Lubavitch Archives, one of the largest digital archives of Chabad-Lubavitch photographs and documents, for supplying many of the book's illustrations.

The final section of this book includes a glimpse into the life of our uncle, our father's brother, dear friend, and business partner, Yosef Yitzchak Deitsch, alav hashalom. You will also find highlights of the too-short lives of our dear brothers, Levi Yitzchak and Nosson Nota Deitsch, aleihem hashalom, both of whom we miss more deeply with each passing day.

We are forever thankful to Hashem for granting us the presence of the Rebbe, who continues to guide us in how to live more meaningful and purposeful lives.

May we merit the revelation of *Moshiach Tzidkeinu* . . . now!

The Deitsch Family

[Part I]

Roots

JOURNEY TO
FREEDOM

I n 1946, at the request of the Polish government, the Soviet Union opened its borders to allow Polish fugitives from World War II to return home. Chabad-Lubavitch Chassidim, suffering under Communist persecution of religion, seized the opportunity and began forging Polish papers. By establishing an underground network for the forgeries and bribing government officials, many Chassidim were able to escape the USSR. But the gratuitous cruelty of some Soviet officials and the suspicion of the Poles made the journey extremely dangerous.

Among the Chabad Chassidim who fled were Sholom and Mirel Deitsch. The fact that Mirel was then expecting their first child did not prevent the couple from embarking on the arduous journey of over three thousand miles from Samarkand, Uzbekistan, to the Polish border. Lodging was arranged for them in the city of Lvov (known in German as Lemberg), Ukraine.

Mirel gave birth to a baby boy on 11 Cheshvan 5707 (November 5, 1946). At his *bris*, eight days later, the baby was named Zalman Yuda after his maternal great-grandfather, a Chassid who had been a wealthy lumber merchant.

News of the birth breathed joy into the Chassidim on the run. A few even made their way to the Deitsches' lodging for the bris with the fervent hope that this

Mirel holding baby Zalman.

LIBRARY OF AGUDAS CHASSIDEI CHABAD

would be the last time they would have to celebrate such an occasion in secret. Weeping tears of joy, Mirel told the assembled, "I brought another Jewish soul into the world and entered him into the covenant of Avraham."

Life in the border town was perilous. Local families would agree to provide lodging for the refugees only for a steep fee. "If the authorities would find locals hiding [refugees] in their homes, their punishment would be severe," wrote Rabbi Zalman Butman, who left the USSR with the Deitsches.

Men with beards did not dare go outdoors during the day, so the young children and adolescents ran errands for them. "Everyone waited in their places with no knowledge of when their next

SHOLOM FRIDLAND

A group of Chassidim gathered in Lvov shortly before smuggling across the border.

step to freedom would come," Rabbi Butman wrote.

Despite the desperate conditions in Lvov, the Chassidim orga-nized an ad hoc *cheder* for their children. Classes were held in the home where the Deitsches were staying. "I was very happy," Mirel wrote in her unpublished autobiography. "My first child was born. The infant was in the same room with the cheder boys." She was sure, she wrote, that he had "absorbed something" from the holy atmosphere created by their Torah study.

The years would prove her right. A resolute young man whose love of Torah was combined with a passion for kindness inherited from his grandparents, Zalman Yuda Deitsch would go on to lead an extraordinary life.

LEGACY OF KINDNESS

Sholom's parents, Mendel and Hinda Deitsch, were renowned for their kindness and hospitality. The family at first lived in Mendel's hometown of Dokshytsy, Belarus, and later moved to Kharkov, Ukraine. During World War II, as the Germans made their way toward Kharkov, the Deitsches successfully obtained train tickets and fled east.

(Shortly after they left, the Germans conquered the city in the First Battle of Kharkov [October 1941]. The family later learned that the Jews who had remained behind were terrorized and murdered.)

For the next few weeks, they travelled by train, foot, and other means over two thousand miles to Samarkand, Uzbekistan, where they planned to meet up with other Chabad families. When they arrived, they were greeted not by war, but by hunger. Food was rationed, and citizens were forced to stand on line in the freezing

AVROHOM MOSHE DEITSCH

The Deitsch family in their younger years. Sitting (from left):
Mendel, Sholom, Dovid, Hinda, and Maryasha Rybalchenko.
Standing: Kushya, Hendel, and Mirel Kugel.

cold for hours to collect their meager portions. Young children, the elderly, and those who fell ill faced an impossible choice: risk their lives standing in the brutal cold or stay at home and starve.

Realizing their predicament, Hinda Deitsch and her daughters-in-law began to collect ration cards from those who could not leave their homes. They would pass through the lines multiple times each day to collect food on behalf of others, placing themselves in grave danger of being recognized and arrested.

They brought any extra food to their home and placed it in a large pot, added water, and cooked it into a porridge, which they served to anyone who asked. Their house was always packed with hungry people, and they made sure everyone left with renewed strength. There was a goat outside the house, Mirel recalled, who welcomed all the visitors. "From the yard there were lines of people with bowls in their hands."

Though it was Mendel's job to organize the distribution of

porridge, he refused to play the part of the benevolent host. He and the children would wait on line for their portions along with everyone else while one of the guests served and received the thanks.[1]

Rabbi Guttman Baras.

Among those who benefited from the Deitsches' kindness were Gershon Ber Jacobson, later the editor of the *Algemeiner Journal,* and Rabbi Guttman Baras, who would become a *mohel.* An orphan, Rabbi Baras treated the Deitsches as if they were his parents. He performed many brisin for their children and grandchildren in the United States.

Another one of the "steady guests" was the young orphan Hayshke Dubrawsky, who was then ill with typhus, which was a deadly epidemic at the time. The Deitsches brought him to live in their attic, away from the others. Mendel would go upstairs and patiently feed him, spoonful by spoonful, slowly reviving him and bringing him back to good health. Hinda would also go from hospital to hospital looking for Jewish patients and bring them pre-

1. Retold for children by their granddaughter Rochel Sandman in *Perfect Porridge* and *As Big as an Egg.*

cious bread, giving them strength to overcome their illnesses.

Among many other virtues, Mendel and Hinda bequeathed to their children, Yekusiel, Chana Devorah, Maryasha, Mirel, Chanoch Hendel, Dovid Shlomo, Sholom Yeshaya, and Dusya, their exceptional generosity and a passionate desire to do good.

Childhood

Born in Kharkov in 1918, Sholom entered a family that was suffering doubly under Communist persecution, first because of their identity as religious Jews, and second because of their participation in Chabad's underground campaign to keep Judaism alive in the Soviet Union.

Not much is known about Sholom's childhood. He never spoke about it to his family, and although he expressed a wish to write his life story, he never got to do it.

Sometime in 1944, Sholom became engaged to his cousin Mirel Rubin, the daughter of Mendel and Alta Rubin (nee Deitsch). In Mirel's memoirs of her early years, which she carefully recorded, she describes how her mother continued the Deitsch tradition of opening her home to guests and caring for the sick.

"I remember our clean, cozy house," she wrote. "In the living-dining room, my mother set up a bed and made a divider out of flowers and plants." Behind the divider lodged an old sick man, who would walk around the house saying, "*Abi gezunt.*" Mirel admitted that as a child she had imitated him behind his back. Seven decades later, however, she understood the significance of his simple, oft-repeated request, asking Hashem to "just give us health."

She also recalled that her mother would receive clandestine messages asking her to do various tasks on behalf of the Jewish community "to strengthen *Yiddishkeit.*"

Tragically, when Mirel was seventeen, her mother passed away. But at the time, her sorrow was almost eclipsed by a much larger tragedy in the community: five members of a Jewish family had died in a fire, and their funeral was held at the same time as her mother's.

Mirel was twenty in the winter of 1941, when the Soviets began to draft young men to serve in war. She was enlisted to distribute the draft letters, a job for which, years later, she felt deep remorse—the letters were nothing less than a death certificate for the recipients. "I thought I fulfilled a special patriotic duty, but now that I am many decades older, I feel very, very guilty because maybe, because of me, someone died in the war.... May Hashem forgive me."

In June 1941, shortly after Mirel's twenty-first birthday, the Germans violated the Molotov-Ribbentrop Pact by invading the Soviet Union. As the German army approached her hometown of Leningrad (today St. Petersburg), the Soviets began evacuating pregnant women and small children from the city.

One day, the phone rang in their home. It was Mirel's cousin Yekusiel "Kushe" Deitsch, who lived with his wife in Kharkov. He asked Mirel how they were faring and told her that everything was well with him. But shortly thereafter, he was drafted into the Red Army and died in combat. "I never thought that this would be the last time I would ever speak to him," Mirel wrote.

Mirel's sister Chana, who was married to their cousin Hendel (Sholom's brother) and expecting a baby, made plans to leave the city. Mirel was to accompany her, but their father, Mendel, and Chana's husband would remain in Leningrad. Mirel recalled her last moments with her father. "I hung on the back of my father's chair in my new knitted jacket, kissed him, and we were on the way."

The two sisters went to stay with a relative, Dr. Yosef Shagalowitz, who ran a psychiatric hospital in a small village outside of Gorky. There, Mirel received a letter from Sholom, which she described as an exciting and happy moment during those frightening times. (She did not disclose its contents in her autobiography, however.)

They remained with their relative until Chana gave birth to a baby boy. She wanted to give him a bris, but the doctor, frightened of the Communists, refused to have it performed on the hospital grounds. Instead, from Leningrad, their father arranged for Shlomo

Sholom Deitsch.

AVROHOM MOSHE DEITSCH

Raskin, an activist in the Chabad underground, to perform the circumcision in his home.

"It's hard to understand how this was arranged," Mirel wrote. "Everything had to be done with utmost secrecy—practicing religion was forbidden. No one was allowed to share in our *simchah*— the bris."

The sisters eventually moved to Klukovkah, where Chana's husband, Hendel, joined them. To their horror, however, shortly thereafter he was drafted into the army. Both sisters accompanied him to the conscription office, where Hendel was directed to join the line of departing soldiers. "It was a very difficult departure," Mirel later wrote. "When the line began to move, many women,

The Deitsch family in Samarkand. Sitting (left to right) Dovid Deitsch, Hinda Deitsch, Mendel Deitsch, Yisroel Kugel, and Sholom Deitsch. Standing: Sara Deitsch, Dusia and Mordechai Rivkin, Mirel Kugel, Esther Rochel Paltiel, and Mirel Deitsch.

including myself, followed . . . until it was out of sight."

Fortunately, Hendel was deemed unfit for service because of a bad eye. He returned to Klukovkah where it was decided that they would move deeper into the Soviet Union, away from the war, to Samarkand, Uzbekistan. There they established a somewhat normal existence. Mirel began to attend school again, though she had to travel an hour on foot each way.

Mirel and her sister and brother-in-law were among the more fortunate refugees in the city. Samarkand was full of starving people. On her way to and from school, Mirel passed the marketplace, where people would exchange their most precious belongings for a little food. The market was closed when she passed in the morning, but "at the gate were all the dead bodies" of those who had succumbed to hunger while waiting for it to open, she wrote. "It was an inhumanly dreadful sight."

By that time, having seen so much death and suffering, they were numbed to every emotion—save one. The weather in Samarkand was erratic, very hot during the day and bitterly cold at night. "No one ever felt the weather, though, only the hunger."

During this time, she reunited with her uncle and aunt, Mendel and Hinda, who made the daily soup which fed so many. But it was Hinda's self-sacrifice, Mirel wrote, that made it possible.

Since it was difficult and expensive to use firewood, Hinda would gather donkey manure from the streets, which she mixed with hay and pounded into flat cakes that were dried in the sun for several days. The result, called in Russian *kazyakies*, could be used for fuel. "These kazyakies saved many lives."

Finding a religious spouse was extremely difficult, and when Mirel and Sholom decided to marry, there was great joy in the family. However, their circumstances made it impossible to mark the engagement with much fanfare.

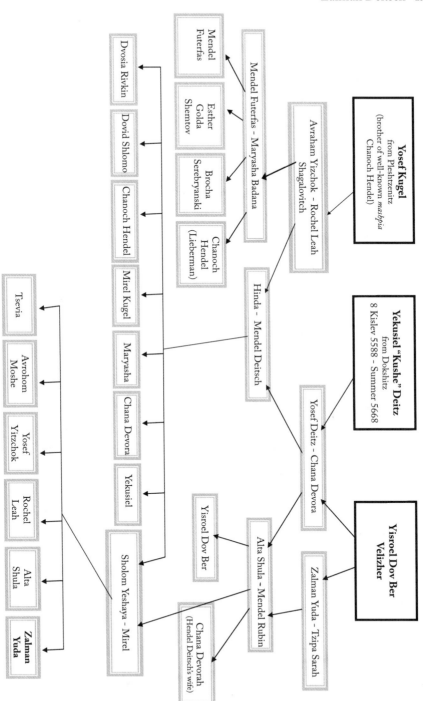

HONEST
TO A FAULT

The parents' grief over Kushe's death was compounded when, shortly after Sholom became engaged, he, too, was called to the draft board. To escape the draft, it was necessary to lie about one's health. But Sholom was not someone who could lie convincingly. The fear in the Deitsch home was palpable.

He would later tell his family what happened during his interview:

Who is your father? *A religious Jew.*

Was your father ever jailed? *Yes.*

Why was he arrested? *He spread Judaism and harbored illegal gold.*

Do you have relatives outside of the Soviet Union? *Yes, in America.*

"One of his personality traits was honesty," Mirel wrote.

The Chelyabinsk prison camp around the time Sholom was there.

Though he knew it would make him a criminal in the eyes of the Soviets, "He decided to answer all questions in truth."

The draft officer told him that they could not enlist him to the frontlines because, "We cannot trust you that you will not betray us."

Sholom was not sent home, however. He was sent to jail, where he found himself in the company of hooligans and hard-core criminals. At first he was not happy that he was separated from his friends, who had been sent to the front, but he soon realized that he was fortunate to have been spared.

While on the front his friends were constantly under enemy fire, in jail, his biggest problem was avoiding harassment from the other inmates. In order to survive, he soon realized he would need to adapt to his surroundings and at least pretend to participate in their rough way of life. "This helped him get into their crowd more easily, and they didn't bother him," Mirel wrote.

Sholom was later sent to the Chelyabinsk labor camp in Siberia. Ostensibly, his job there was to prepare ammunition for the Red Army, but it was almost impossible to work under the conditions. There was little food besides for rotten potatoes. Sometimes even those were scarce.

The prisoners' clothes were tattered, their shoes torn, and there was no heat. With little protection from the freezing weather, they dug an underground basement where they could keep themselves somewhat warm. His fellow inmates once pounced on an animal, divided the meat, and devoured it. Sholom refused to eat the non-kosher meat, however, and exchanged his portion for another rotten potato. He would also exchange his daily soup for a sugar cube.

Even under these conditions, he would secretly *daven* three times a day. Though he was physically malnourished, his wife wrote later, his rich spiritual heritage sustained him. "Through all this, he believed Hashem would pull him through."

Visitors in Chelyabinsk

The letters he wrote to his family were Sholom's only connection to the outside world. When he had been in the labor camp for some time, his mother noticed that his letters took on a depressed tone. As more and more gloomy letters arrived, Hinda became concerned that she would lose a second son. She decided to go visit the labor camp and try to help him in any way possible. At the very least she would raise his spirits.

Her son Dovid obtained a train ticket for her, and shortly after Purim she set out, intending to spend Pesach with him. She left the "soup kitchen" and the children, who were already "older," under the care of her husband.

The train station in Samarkand was packed with people who wanted to leave. A ticket meant nothing, she soon realized. There was no way she would be able to board a train unless she found

Prisoners returning to the Chelyabinsk prison camp, circa 1945.

someone to help her. She approached the station manager, but he simply raised his arms in despair. "See for yourself what is going on here," he told her.

Hinda persisted in her request, however, until finally the manager offered her a deal. The station's bathrooms were filthy, and soon there would be an inspection. "If you will clean the bathrooms," he said, "I will arrange for you to get on the next train."

She immediately agreed. Dismissing her own dignity, she cleaned the disgusting bathrooms until they were sparkling. The manager kept his word and arranged for her to board the next train. It was so crowded that for much of the journey she stood on the steps and held on to the railings for dear life.

In Siberia, she found the Rabin family, who assisted her in determining which camp Sholom was being held in. After walking several hours through the forests in the freezing cold, she arrived at the labor camp. She continued walking, following the barbed-wire fence that marked the perimeter, until, in the distance, she saw a bony figure digging. Her motherly instincts told her it was her son.

Sholom was busy digging a burrow in the snow when he heard his name being called. At first he paid no attention, thinking that it was a daydream. "How good it would be to really hear my mother's voice again," he later recalled thinking.

The calls continued, however, and finally he looked up to see whose voice it was. From afar he saw the shadow of a person who looked like his mother, standing almost waist-deep in the snow. He realized that he was not losing his mind and began slowly walking toward the gate.

They held each other's hands tightly through the fence, crying and soothing each other.

"Mother, where will I take you to stay? I live in an underground mud hut with forty men," Sholom said. She assured him that she already had a place to stay. "I have it all arranged, and we will celebrate Pesach together."

The Rabins were kind people who, though they knew little about Judaism, were willing to lend a hand to their brethren. Hinda koshered their oven and, with flour she had brought with her, baked matzah for Pesach.

Her next task was to arrange for them to be allowed to celebrate together. To her surprise, even the commanders were in despair about the camp's situation. Their uniforms were tattered and their shoes full of holes. After she bribed them with leather and tobacco she brought for that purpose, they let her into the camp.

After Pesach, she made plans to return home. She told the commander that if they sent her son home as soon as possible, she would send them more leather.

After she left, Sholom found that her visit and her words had lifted him out of despair. His will to live was returning, and the hope of one day being free flickered inside of him.

With great difficulty, Hinda had managed to obtain tickets back to Samarkand. However, the return journey proved to be even more dangerous than she had expected. On the train, a kind stranger warned her that bandits were scheming to rob her and throw her off the moving train. She got off at the next stop, but had to wait for many days in the station for another train to arrive.

A young Mirel.

AVROHOM MOSHE DEITSCH

By the time she arrived home, her clothing was tattered, and she had lost a lot of weight. "But she was a woman of great determination," Mirel wrote, "and realizing her obligations [in] helping the poor and sickly," she made every effort to recover quickly.

Over the next few weeks, she regained her strength. The family knew that she was back to herself when she was once again fully involved in her acts of kindness.

That summer, not long after Hinda had returned, Mirel decided that she wanted to visit her fiancé, "with hopes of being able to free Sholom from this torture." With a large amount of money and tobacco, and with faith in her mission, she set off for Chelyabinsk. To catch a train, she sometimes had to remain in a station along the way for a while, a dangerous prospect for a young woman alone.

She arrived a few days before Rosh Hashanah. By then, Sholom, thanks to his mother's bribes, had attained a privileged status in the camp. He was surprised and overjoyed to see his future bride and arranged for her to stay in the camp with an engineer who lived with his ailing mother.

During her visit, Mirel asked to meet with the camp's work manager and bribed him with gifts to free Sholom as soon as possible. A few days later, she began her journey home, once more sleeping in train stations, wondering if she would make it home alive. She finally arrived in Samarkand, where she learned that a week after she had departed the camp, Sholom had been freed and was on the way home.

Even this good news was accompanied with pain, however, for around the same time, she learned that her father had disappeared.

On a freezing day during the Siege of Leningrad, when, because of the German blockade on the city, hunger, cold, and even cannibalism were commonplace, Mendel Rubin had been seen going to the market to exchange his shoes for a piece of bread. He never returned. "We can assume he died of cold, hunger, or robbery," his daughter wrote. The family never found out where he was buried, though it was likely a mass grave.

A few days after Sholom's arrival in Samarkand, on the eve of Sukkos 5705 (1944), the couple married. "Even though a war was raging, we had a *freilech*, beautiful wedding," Mirel wrote. In attendance were many of the Chassidim in Samarkand, who thanked G-d for the marriage and the groom's freedom. For the next twenty-three years, on Shemini Atzeres, Sholom and Mirel held a grand celebration to mark their marriage and Sholom's liberation.

A year after the wedding, the entire Deitsch family embarked on their journey to freedom.

UNCERTAIN JOURNEY

T he Deitsches remained in Lvov for close to a month after Zalman was born. It was dangerous to stay but perhaps even more dangerous to go. Finally, a group of Chassidim resolved to leave, reasoning that there was a small chance they might make it, whereas if they stayed where they were, they were certainly doomed.

A group of thirty-seven people made their way over the border into Poland with hope and a prayer. After arriving safely, they immediately sent a telegram to those in Lvov hinting at their success. The Chassidim breathed a sigh of relief, and another group of fifty-seven, including the Deitsches, began making preparations to leave. Forged passports were distributed with fictitious family names. Mirel became the daughter of Mrs. Esther Feldman.

It turned out that the only train the group could take would depart on Friday evening. The Chassidim were greatly pained.

Soviet soldiers outside of the Lvov train station.

Having guarded the holy day with self-sacrifice in the Soviet Union—many had even been thrown into prison for refusing to work or to send their children to school on Shabbos—were they now to desecrate it in order to escape? The rabbis in Lvov ruled that this was a life-and-death matter. The Communists were brutal murderers who would not hesitate to throw them and their families in prison if they were discovered. Under the circumstances, it was not only permissible to travel on Shabbos, but it was incumbent upon them to do so.

Thus, the group headed to the *vokzal*, the train station, which was heavily guarded and therefore dangerous for them. The secret police and the Red Army swarmed the station, in addition to the many informers among the passengers and staff.

To get to the station, the elderly and the young children with their mothers rode on a truck while those who could walk made every effort not to desecrate the Shabbos. "It was very depressing," Mirel wrote, "because we all felt guilty travelling on Shabbos."

On the train, they squeezed into cars among hundreds of other passengers. The minutes before departure ticked slowly by while the terrified Chassidim imagined that they were about to be dragged from the train at any moment by the secret police. Indeed, one of the Chassidim and several others were arrested.

Finally, the steam engine blew its whistle, and the train lurched into the darkness. The organizers of the group immediately began reviewing each member's new identity, siblings, and birth dates. "We were all very tense," Mirel wrote of the time they spent on the train. "With great miracles I managed to keep my son Zalman alive. In this very carriage, a not-so-lucky baby was smothered to death."

At the border, the train stopped and everyone was ordered to get off. "We had to stand in the cold winter air, frozen to the bone, for almost two hours until we were allowed back [on the train]," recalled Moishe Levertov in his autobiography, *The Man Who Mocked the KGB*. "A guard came aboard to question us. Standing in the middle of our car, he read our names from a list, asking us to identify ourselves."

When a young girl responded correctly to her alias, Mr. Levertov wrote, the guard was surprised. "Very good!" he said sarcastically. "She has learned well." Most of the group made it across the border.

When they arrived in Poland, they boarded trucks, which were so crowded that another child passed away during the ride to Krakow. Mirel protected Zalman fiercely with her life. When they arrived, they were taken to a building where other refugees were housed. They were not safe yet, however. Many Poles were antisemites, and though the war was over, they were still murdering Jews. Many survivors of the concentration camps who returned home were killed by their former neighbors.

In Krakow, Zalman reached his thirtieth day of life, the oc-

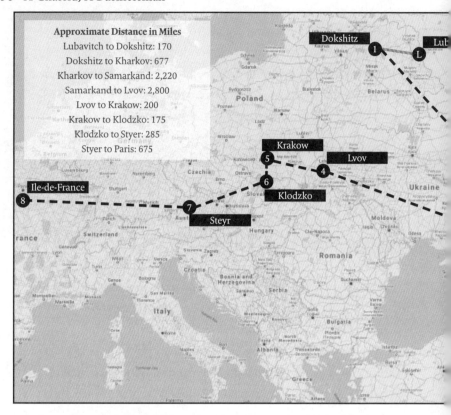

Approximate Distance in Miles
Lubavitch to Dokshitz: 170
Dokshitz to Kharkov: 677
Kharkov to Samarkand: 2,220
Samarkand to Lvov: 2,800
Lvov to Krakow: 200
Krakow to Klodzko: 175
Klodzko to Styer: 285
Styer to Paris: 675

casion for his *pidyon haben*. Hinda went to the marketplace; purchased a chicken, a turkey, and bread; and prepared a feast. It was an occasion for doubled joy as the Chassidim also celebrated their freedom from their Soviet oppressors. "There were many people and much overcrowding," Mirel wrote. "There were many Lubavitchers as well as Polish Jews with us. Even so, it was a very happy time, and many people even became drunk."

The Journey Continues

After a short respite, the group now began the second leg of their journey, going for days without any basic provisions or rest. When they arrived at their next destination, the town of Klodzko in southwestern Poland, dust had gathered on Zalman's face. The discomfort and lack of privacy had begun grating on the refugees'

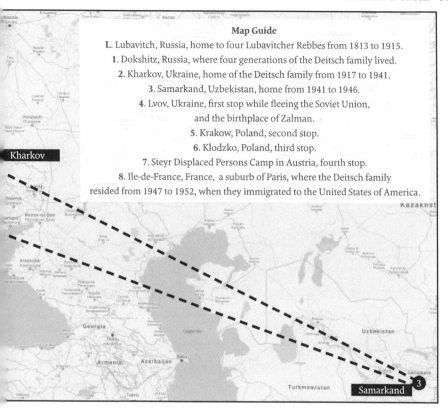

Map Guide

L. Lubavitch, Russia, home to four Lubavitcher Rebbes from 1813 to 1915.

1. Dokshitz, Russia, where four generations of the Deitsch family lived.

2. Kharkov, Ukraine, home of the Deitsch family from 1917 to 1941.

3. Samarkand, Uzbekistan, home from 1941 to 1946.

4. Lvov, Ukraine, first stop while fleeing the Soviet Union, and the birthplace of Zalman.

5. Krakow, Poland, second stop.

6. Klodzko, Poland, third stop.

7. Steyr Displaced Persons Camp in Austria, fourth stop.

8. Ile-de-France, France, a suburb of Paris, where the Deitsch family resided from 1947 to 1952, when they immigrated to the United States of America.

nerves.

One night, Zalman woke up in the large hall where they were sleeping and began to wail. His mother rocked him, fed him, and soothed him, but nothing worked. The crying was just getting louder. Soon many people woke up and began to complain. Night was their one time of comfort, when their bodies rested and their minds were relieved from constant worry.

Mrs. Mirel Kugel, Sholom's sister, who was nearby, took Zalman into her arms and began to caress him. As she moved her hand over his head, she realized that a large louse was digging its legs into his scalp. She got rid of the bug, and he immediately ceased crying.

Their next stop was a displaced persons camp, which was

SHOLOM FRIDLAND

A group of Chassidim in an Austrian displaced persons camp.

nothing more than a former concentration camp. They were surrounded by barbwire, and smoke spewed from the chimneys, giving the refugees headaches; there was no heat and food was scarce. "We all suffered from the cold and hunger," Mirel wrote. "But we were all happy because we had torn ourselves away from behind the Iron Curtain."

From there they moved on to the Steyr Displaced Persons Camp in Austria. Things were a little better there. They had their own private room in a hut, where there were beds. Sholom built a table and bench for them, which became a running family joke for years—the table was too low and the bench was too high.

The young couple was now able to give their baby son more attention, but there was little food to nourish their starving bodies. The Chassidim were becoming despondent. One survivor of the hunger during the infamous Siege of Leningrad told everyone that he was afraid that some wouldn't survive the shortage of food in the DP camp.

Zalman in France.

A little food did arrive via relief organizations, but much of it was not kosher. Under the circumstances, some Jews in the camp found ways to justify eating it, but the Chassidim absolutely refused to touch it. Once, the Joint Distribution Committee ("the Joint") distributed bottles of oil to all the refugees. Because the kosher status of the oil was questionable, the Chassidim stayed away from it too.

The situation was so bad that when a nurse saw how scrawny Zalman was, she wrapped some sugar in a thin cloth and let the baby suck on it. Soon it was discovered that he had a stomach infection. A doctor told Mirel and Sholom that he had to be hospitalized right away.

The only hospital available at the time was a German one. Mirel did not want to place her child in the hands of German doctors without being there to observe, so she got herself admitted for fictitious reasons. In the hospital, she kept her eyes on her baby. "In the middle of the night I'd hide in the shadows in his ward, quietly

The Previous Rebbe.

standing vigil over my child."

One night, a German doctor discovered her by the baby's bed and made the connection. "I knew you didn't trust me!" he said. "This is because I am German, no?"

After mother and baby were discharged, perhaps seeking to prove his good intentions, the doctor offered that if Mirel would bring Zalman to his personal clinic, he would do everything he could to help him. But Mirel, still wary, refused the offer, "Of course I never went to see him."

In New York, the Previous Rebbe had founded Aid for Refugees (Ezras Plitim V'siduram), later known as the European Bureau of Chabad-Lubavitch, or Lishka (Bureau) for short. As its head, he appointed the activist Rabbi Binyomin Eliyahu Gorodetsky, whose office was in Paris. Among its activities on behalf of Holocaust survivors and refugees was to arrange permanent resettlement for the Chassidim who left the Soviet Union.

When Rabbi Gorodetsky heard reports of the food shortage in the Austrian DP camp, he immediately began working to have the group moved to Paris. The French government, however, was unwilling to accept refugees, even on a short-term basis.

"How much pain and anguish I suffered over these few weeks," he wrote to the Previous Rebbe. "I waited every day for their arrival from Austria." His concern that they might not arrive was compounded by the worry that he had not yet found a place for them to live.

When spring arrived, things began to look positive. Papers were finally obtained for the first group of fifty-eight travelers. "I had to employ two people," Rabbi Gorodetsky wrote. "One in Paris to work on obtaining the visas, and one in Austria to take care of all the papers that were needed from those receiving the visas."

On Friday, 12 Iyar 5707 (May 2, 1947), the refugees finally arrived in Paris, where a bus was waiting to take them to the Eiffel

Sholom (front, left) at a farbrengen in a DP camp in France.

One of the French mansions leased by the Joint for the Lubavitch refugees.

Mansion in the suburb of Ile-de-France. "The entire mansion is empty. It has rooms, beds, and all that is needed in an apartment," Rabbi Gorodetsky wrote to the Rebbe. He reported that the busses had arrived and everyone had organized themselves. "It has a place for Torah study, and every area has a stove to cook."

The mansion was surrounded by lush greenery, which brought much respite to the exhausted refugees. The Deitsches received a room with a bath and a porch. The bathroom and kitchen they shared with others. They were given from two to three o'clock in the afternoon to use the kitchen.

When the good news reached the Previous Rebbe, he wrote to the group's leaders (*Igros Kodesh*, vol. 9, letter 3,041):

> In response to your letter about the arrival of *anash* from the first camp in Austria to Paris, I thank G-d for the great kindness He did with you until now. May His kindness remain with you forever.
>
> Surely you will all remember the holy mission that divine

providence placed on each one of you: to bring light to every place that you come to. The light of Torah and *Chassidus*, the strengthening of Torah and Judaism in general, and especially Jewish education, with brotherly love and proper virtues.

Please send my greetings to all of the refugees, may they be well. Hashem should assist you in organizing your lives for the good, and bless you with success in all that you need, materially and spiritually.

The refugees sent their older children to the new yeshiva in Brunoy, France, and a playgroup was started for the younger ones by Ms. Shifra Perman (later Swerdlov), who lovingly taught them about Yiddishkeit and the way of Chassidus.

Now, for the first time since they had left Samarkand, they had to support themselves. There were very few options, and Sholom decided to join his brother Dovid in making wine and selling it in the Pletzel, the Jewish quarter in Paris. His income was not much, but it was better than nothing. "We began to set up some semblance of normal living," Mirel wrote.

PERMANENT HOME

Immediately, the Chassidim began making plans to find more permanent situations. Most of them wanted to move to New York to be near the Rebbe, whom they had not seen in years, or, as in Mirel and Sholom's case, had never seen at all. The Previous Rebbe, however, had other plans for many of them. He wanted his Chassidim to settle around the world in order to spread Judaism and Chassidus.

All of Sholom's paternal uncles already lived in America. Shmuel "Sam" lived in Springfield, Massachusetts; his half brother, Zalman Isser "Sol" Deitz, lived in Norwalk, Connecticut, where Sol ran a tie store; also in Norwalk was Monne "Manuel," who had a small hardware store; Nochum "Norman" lived in the Bronx, New York, and had a business in the garment district. They and their families had immigrated together with their aunt, their father's sister Tzivie Leiberman, some fifty years earlier. Tzivie lived

Sholom and Mirel holding Zalman and newborn Alta Shula in France, 1948.

in Hartford, Connecticut. With the help of Sol, Sholom's elderly parents were able to move to Norwalk in 1947 and were followed shortly afterward by two of their married children, Dovid and Sarah Deitsch and Dusya and Mordechai Rivkin. In 1949, Mendel traveled to Crown Heights and spent Rosh Hashanah with the Previous Rebbe.

Sholom and Mirel sent a letter to the Previous Rebbe asking where they should go to live. Receiving no answer, they remained in France. Over the next two years, the couple had two more children. Alta Shula, born on the second night of Chanukah in 1947, named after her maternal grandmother, was followed eighteen months later by Rochel Leah, named for her paternal great-grandmother. The two sisters, so close in age, became best friends and were often mistaken for twins. Their joy in each other's company created a lively and happy atmosphere in the Deitsch home.

On the 10th of Shevat 5710 (1950), the couple mourned the passing of the Previous Rebbe, whom they had never met. A year later, they celebrated when his son-in-law formally accepted leadership of the Chabad movement. It was under the new Rebbe's guidance that they finally made efforts to obtain entry visas to the United States.

The Rebbe shortly after he formally accepted leadership in 1951.

They named their son, who was born shortly before Rosh Hashanah, on 23 Elul 5711 (September 24, 1951), Yosef Yitzchok, after the Previous Rebbe.

[Part II]

New World

AMERICAN
CHALLENGE

The visas arrived, and the young Deitsch family began preparing for their last long journey, the one that would bring them to their final destination. America was the land of freedom and opportunity. They could live as religious Jews without fear. It would be the realization of the dream for which they had risked their lives by fleeing the Soviet Union.

The famed Chassid Reb Peretz Mochkin sent them off with a warning, however: "Be watchful over your children in America, for there they will have to contend with many [spiritual] difficulties, and their life tribulations are still before them."

Sholom's father wrote from Connecticut, telling them that even once they arrived, they would have to pass a difficult border review and exam. He advised them to dress the children well. The Americans were worried that immigrants would become charity cases, so families that gave the impression of being well-to-do had a greater chance of entering the country.

On the day of departure, the Deitsches arrived at the pier dressed in their finest clothes, including fur coats for the mother and children. But when they tried to board the ship, they were told that children under the age of one were not allowed to travel. The border patrol officer informed them matter-of-factly that they would have to remain in a camp until their son Yosef's first birthday.

Zalman, age two.

The family was sprayed with DDT, a chemical used at the time to control malaria and typhus, both deadly epidemics after the war. Their food was confiscated in case it was "contaminated." Though they were allowed to be together during the day, at night, the children were given a small room to be with their mother while Sholom was assigned to a building for men. Adequate food was provided, but Sholom and Mirel refused to eat anything besides basic bread.

After a month of living without knowing what the next day would bring, they were suddenly told to gather their belongings

AVROHOM MOSHE DEITSCH

Sholom and Mirel with their children (from left): Alta, Zalman, and Rochel Leah.

and go to the airport. In the rush they had to leave some things behind, but they did not forget Reb Mendel's instruction to dress the children well.

At the airport, the border control officers selected the "wealthy" family decked in fur for an additional search, fearing they might be trying to smuggle expensive items out of the country. Mirel would retell how, after searching thoroughly, the officers were disappointed to find only a piece of butter she had taken to feed the children. "A rich family and this is what you have with you?"

They were the last to board the plane, which had only three seats left for the family of six. Zalman and Alta sat in one, Mirel held Yosef, and Sholom held Rochel Leah. Shortly after the plane took off, Alta disappeared while Rochel Leah began to wail from fright. Sholom calmed her and held the baby while Mirel searched the plane for Alta. She was having no success, when suddenly the young girl emerged from the cockpit. "My brave explorer," Mirel wrote.

En route to New York, the plane was diverted to Canada, where they were given a hotel room to stay in until they could continue to their final destination. There they had a shower, a luxury after a month in the camp.

Due to the language barrier, the family at times struggled to follow instructions from the Canadian officials. They were told to board a bus to the airport, though it was so crowded that there

Mendel and Hinda Deitsch (sitting) with brothers (left to right) Sol, Monne, and Norman Deitz.

were no more seats available. In the chaos, Zalman was left behind. Mirel only realized what had happened as the bus pulled out, and she began to wail (she did not speak any English yet), motioning with her hands to tell the driver what had happened. Later, she tried to describe the terror she felt at that moment. "Only one who [has been] forcefully separated from their child can understand." She described the incident in her autobiography, writing, "Oh, Hashem! How good to be together! Something not to be taken for granted."

At the airport, the well-dressed children caught the attention

The Deitsch siblings, 1954. Clockwise: Yosef, Zalman, Rochel Leah, and Alta.

of two businessmen, who offered to take them to a café and buy them treats. The Deitsches thanked them but declined, saying they only ate kosher food. "Don't worry, we know what kosher is," the men promised. Reb Peretz's warning still echoing in their ears, the couple anxiously looked on as the men bought the children soda and sweets.

When they finally arrived in New York, their uncles Sol and Sam were waiting at the airport, accompanied by representatives of the Joint. It was New Year's, 1953, and the Joint had sponsored dolls for the children, an expensive gift at the time. But Zalman refused his doll and threw a tantrum until someone caught on and brought him a ball. "This is America laughing," Mirel wrote.

The three-story building in Norwalk, Connecticut, where Mendel, Hinda, and Sol lived together became the Deitsches' first home in America. There, in a small apartment on the third floor, they were able to recover from their ordeal in peace and privacy.

NOTHING FOR GRANTED

Everything about their new home seemed impossibly luxurious to the children. The apartment had a bath, a dining room, and two bedrooms. There was even a backyard where they could play.

Family members and their friends gave the new immigrants used furniture and basic appliances. For a couch, they had a mattress on two boxes with a few pillows on top. The children used it as a trampoline during the day, while at night it often accommodated people who needed a place to stay. One young man had escaped the Soviet Union and travelled to the United States via France and London. He needed much support and spent several weeks in their home. The couple found the space for him in their small apartment, gave him hearty homemade meals, uplifted his spirits, and provided for his material needs.

Food was limited to basics. Whenever they walked past a fruit

Mendel and Hinda with their grandchildren.

store, Mirel would hurry the children by so that they wouldn't feel deprived. The newspaper that the Shabbos fish had been wrapped in was saved for the children to draw on. They would later say they never understood why their coloring paper had a stench of fish.

"Writing books, furniture, clothes, and bananas were not part of our budget," Mirel wrote. Nevertheless, "They were good years. The house was always bubbling over with dancing and singing and laughing."

Soon the family was blessed with another child, whom they named Avrohom Moshe, after Sholom's maternal grandfather, Avrohom Yitzchok, and Mirel's uncle Moshe.

Finding employment was not easy, especially for someone who did not work on Shabbos, but Sholom's commitment to Yiddishkeit never wavered. At one point, he took a job as a truck driver. Whenever he left the city bounds, he would pull over, put on his *gartel*, and say *Tefilas Haderech* word for word (see *Shulchan Aruch, Orach Chayim* 110:4). Every morning he went to the *mik-*

vah, and on Shabbos he woke up extra early to be *ma'aver* the *sedra*.

Although his formal Jewish education had been cut short by the Communist regime, Sholom took every opportunity to participate in Torah shiurim. Once, during a yechidus, private audience, the Rebbe asked him if he studied *Chitas* daily. He responded that he studied the Chumash and recited the daily Tehillim, but that he did not study *Tanya* because he found it hard to understand. The Rebbe advised him to acquire a *Tanya* in Yiddish. From then on, he was careful to complete the full study regimen each day.

At one point, Sol, seeing his nephew's business capabilities, hired him to manage a local tie factory, a role in which he flourished. Despite their newfound "wealth," Sholom and Mirel knew they were starting from scratch and saved every penny from their meager earnings.

EDUCATIONAL DILEMMA

Now that Sholom had a steady job, the couple faced the problem of how to educate their children. At the time, there were few thriving Jewish communities outside of New York. In Norwalk, the only options were public schools or a day school with a very limited Jewish curriculum.

At first, Zalman studied with his grandfather Reb Mendel. But then social services visited the new immigrants' home and told them that by law he had to be enrolled in a school. If he were not registered immediately, the social worker warned, there would be serious consequences.

After much discussion, and a consultation with the Rebbe, they decided to send their eight-year-old son to study in Crown Heights. One night, Sholom packed up Zalman's few articles of clothing and took him to the home of Rabbi Mendel Tenenbaum, the principal of the Lubavitch Yeshivah, which was then located on the corner of Bedford Avenue and Dean Street. Zalman was accepted at the school, and he boarded at the home of Yisroel and Riva Minkowitz. He slept in the same room as their son Meir, who was his age. The two went to yeshiva together each day.

Still, Zalman, age eight, was very young to be living away from home. "Zalman was in Brooklyn, and

Zalman during his time at the Lubavitch Yeshiva on Bedford Avenue and Dean Street, 1956.

the rest of the family was in Norwalk," Mirel wrote of that short period. "This physical separation made him feel like a stranger to us when he visited home. We missed him and he missed us."

One winter afternoon, when it was already getting dark, he came back to Crown Heights alone during a snowstorm. Not recognizing the area under the blanket of white, he got off the bus at the wrong stop and, unable to find the Minkowitzes' house, began to wander aimlessly in the unfamiliar neighborhood.

"A feeling of his father saved him," Mirel recalled. Acting on impulse, "Sholom drove in from Norwalk to visit Zalman after work that day." As he was driving the Crown Heights streets, he

The Rebbe during a farbrengen around the time Tsevie was born.

spotted a small figure—it was his son, standing alone in the dark and the snow.

This episode was a turning point. After much deliberation they decided that something would have to change. They moved once again, this time to Crown Heights, home to the Rebbe and Lubavitch World Headquarters, known as 770. "Our children could now go to Jewish schools, be in the right atmosphere, and live together with our great, revered Rebbe," Mirel wrote.

A Better Life

A new era began for the Deitsch family when they moved to Crown Heights. Sholom regularly attended the Rebbe's *farbrengens*, Chassidic gatherings, making an effort to participate from the beginning to the end, even if it was in the wee hours of the morning. He was at a farbrengen the night Mirel went into labor with their youngest child. Knowing how special those times were to him, she refused to have him notified during the gathering and instead turned to a neighbor, Mrs. Sonia Kaplan, who went with her

Zalman (center) with his siblings at the *upshernish*
of his brother Avraham Moshe (second from right).

to the hospital. When he returned home, Sholom was informed of
the good news. They named their daughter Tsevie, after an aunt
Tzivie Leiberman, who lived in Hartford, Conneticut.

Once again, Sholom needed to find a way to support their
family. He started a business recycling the leftover scraps that
textile companies, which sold only large rolls of material, would
otherwise discard. He sorted through the smaller pieces and sold
them cheaply to companies that could use them. From an early
age, Zalman, when needed, would occasionally assist his father
with the business during his time off from yeshiva.

The company was successful. True to their upbringing, the
Deitsches immediately began using their resources to help others.
Sholom would return from *shul* on Shabbos and yom tov with a
large group of guests. "Let's put everything on the table," he would
tell his wife.

If there was not enough for everyone, he would go to the pantry and bring out anything he found. Soon the Deitsch home became known as a place where one could find a good meal and a lively farbrengen.

The Deitsches had finally settled down. They would remain fixtures in the Crown Heights community for the rest of their lives. "In all our travels, many of them fraught with perils to life itself," Mirel wrote, "our entire group had many questions: Where will we end up? Will we all make it there in one piece? How will we eat? Survive the cold? And many more questions. But we had a wonderful Guide who took care of us even when we felt alone. . . . This was Hashem."

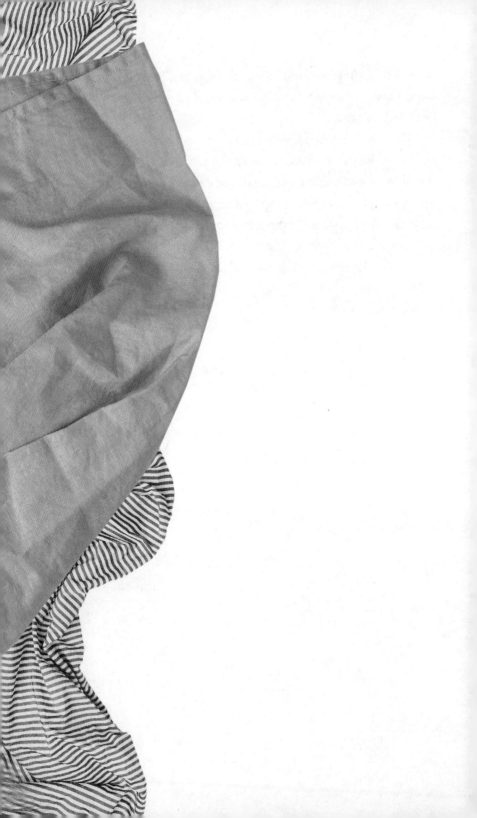

Part III

Young Man

STUDY AND KINDNESS

More than anything else, Zalman remembered his parents' kindness to others. He often told stories of their good deeds; there were two that were particularly instructive.

Rabbi Nissan Nemenov, the famed *mashpia* from the yeshiva in Brunoy, France, once came to New York to spend time close to the Rebbe. He also did some fundraising for the yeshiva during his stay and visited the Deitsch home to ask for their support. At the time, however, the couple did not have the amount that Sholom wanted to give to the yeshiva, which caused him anguish.

Seeing his pain, Mirel took $200, a large sum in those times, out of a hiding place and gave it to Reb Nissan. When Sholom asked her later where she had gotten the money, she told him that for months she had saved a little each week from the allowance he gave her for household items, hoping to eventually purchase a

Rabbi Nissan Nemenov.

kitchen table and chairs.

The second story took place on a Friday evening. The custom at 770 was that the *gabai* announced all the names of those getting married that week and where their *ufruf kiddush* would be. The event was usually hosted by the groom's parents. One week, an orphan that Sholom knew was getting married, and he noticed that his name was not mentioned. Sholom got up on the *bimah* and announced that the *chassan's* kiddush would be at the Deitsch home, 669 Crown Street.

Since everyone knew that a kiddush at the Deitsches' would be a joyous event, many people came. Mirel took out all the food she had in the house and happily set the table. The kiddush was the talk of the town for a long time afterward.

From a young age, Zalman began to emulate his parents' ways. Yankel Goldstein was a young boy when his parents, who lived in Cincinnati, Ohio, sent him to study at the Lubavitch Yeshivah. The couple he boarded with did not speak English, and he found it hard to communicate with them, let alone express his thoughts and feelings.

Yankel sat next to Zalman in class, and they soon became good friends. Zalman would bring him home, where the Deitsch family welcomed him as one of their own. He was soon spending much of his free time there and just going to the other house to sleep.

Yankel related that he could not count the number of times Sholom asked him if he had any money. The answer was usually no, and Sholom would give him some. Zalman later became Yankel's brother-in-law when he married Cyrel, Yankel's wife's sister.

Only Torah

In the mid-1950s, the Rebbe spoke strongly against *chachmas chitzoiniyos* (general studies) for young children. Torah should be the only thing children learn, certainly until the age of nine, and preferably until age twelve or not at all, the Rebbe said. "The first three years of education are the most important for their future success, and here you sully his mind with English, grammar, and the like. Hashem wants to dwell in the mind of the child, and here you take the brain and fill it with other subjects."

The Rebbe said that there was no reason for young children to be preparing to earn a livelihood. The future was up to Hashem. At the end of the day, no one knows the future. When the time would come, they would need to make an effort to make a living, but there was no reason for it to be part of a young child's education.

"Hashem gave us the Torah more than three thousand years ago," the Rebbe said, "and we see that the 'good-for-nothing' nation that does not learn grammar is still holding strong."

After this talk, several parents asked the yeshiva to create a track with only Torah studies. Zalman, who had heard about the talk, asked to join that track. His father, though, wondered if his

The Lubavitch yeshiva on Bedford Avenue and Dean Street.

son was up to it.

He sat Zalman down for a talk. "Why do you want to join that track?" he asked. "Is it because you are lazy? Or because of peer pressure from your friends?"

Zalman responded that he truly wanted to learn only Torah all day. This brought great nachas to his father, who told him, "If the request is coming because you recognize the importance of Torah learning, transfer immediately to the new track."

DEDICATED STUDENT

Zalman's bar mitzvah was celebrated in the dimly lit basement of the Deitsch home. He later recalled how the table was made of a slab of wood propped on two pedestals. There was only a small number of guests, including some illustrious Chassidim, but there was great joy as the Deitsches' eldest son sat next to his grandfather Reb Mendel, who had suffered so much during his life, and repeated a maamar from memory. His grandfather then gave a meaningful speech about what the day meant to him.

After his bar mitzvah, Zalman dedicated himself even more fiercely to Torah study, shying away from the tumult on the streets of New York. After a full day at yeshiva, he continued to learn at a local shul with his study partner, Rabbi Manis Friedman. "We would study, many times until early in the morning," Rabbi Friedman recalled.

AVROHOM MOSHE DEITSCH

At the bar mitzvah of his brother Avrohom Moshe.

Rabbi Friedman also recalled how one night they became so involved in what they were learning that they forgot to daven *maariv*. The next evening, in the middle of his Chassidus class, Reb Yoel Kahan, the mashpia in the yeshiva, told a story about the famed Chassid Reb Gershon Ber of Pahar.

After listening to a maamar delivered by the fourth Chabad Rebbe, the Rebbe Maharash, Reb Gershon Ber would meditate for hours. "He would sit under a tree, with his eyes closed, lost in thought, until he had absorbed the message of the maamar deep in his heart," Reb Yoel said, noting that in this state the Chassid was oblivious of the world around him.

The Rebbe Maharash and his son Rabbi Sholom Dovber, who would become the next Rebbe, were once travelling through Reb Gershon Ber's city when the Chassid was already an elderly man, Reb Yoel continued. Reb Gershon Ber gave his room and bed to the Rebbe while he shared a room with the Rebbe's son.

That night, Rabbi Sholom Dovber watched the elderly Chassid recite *Krias Shema al Hamitah*. When Reb Gershon Ber reached the words *"Lo ashuv oid lehachisecha"* (Neither shall I again anger You), he began to cry bitterly.

The next day, Rabbi Sholom Dovber told his father what he had observed. The Rebbe Maharash thought for some time in silence. Then he told his son why Reb Gershon Ber was crying. Years earlier, Reb Gershon Ber had been sitting under a tree on Shabbos afternoon contemplating the

Rabbi Manis Friedman.

maamar he had just heard. When he finally roused himself, he realized that it was already the morning and that he had not davened maariv. "On this lost maariv, he still cries every night while saying those words," the Rebbe Maharash concluded.

After this story, Reb Yoel returned to the maamar they were learning.

It wasn't until that moment, Rabbi Friedman said, that he realized that he and Zalman had missed maariv the night before. He turned to look at his friend. "Zalman never showed much emotion, but at that moment, he was sitting with his hands covering his eyes, tears rolling down his face."

"Know-It-Alls"

Before the bar mitzvah of Zalman's younger brother Avrohom Moshe, the family was scheduled for a private audience with the Rebbe. Zalman and Yosef were already young men in yeshiva then, and when their father asked them to accompany the family, they demurred, saying that they felt they were not spiritually ready to enter the audience.

In the end, they agreed to come to 770 and waited in the hallway outside the Rebbe's study while the rest of the family went in.

When the Rebbe asked where the two older boys were, Sholom responded that they were not ready for an audience with the Rebbe. "Nu, they are *saam sapozhneks?*" the Rebbe asked with a smile.

This term had entered the Chabad lexicon due to a story that the Rebbe Rayatz once told during a talk (*Sefer Hasichos* 5698, p. 264): A Russian shoemaker once found a pair of *tefillin* and decided to sell them. Being a shoemaker, he assumed that the leather straps were the valuable part of the object and carried them like that, dragging the boxes on the ground. A Jew met him and, horrified at the treatment these sacred objects were receiving, asked where he had gotten them. *"Ya saam sapozhnek"* (I am a shoemaker), the man replied, implying that he had made them himself.

We all make decisions thinking that we're experts, the Rebbe Rayatz concluded. In truth, though, if we do not look up to our mentors, teachers, and elders, often we are no better than this ignorant shoemaker and make more of ourselves than we really are.

It appears that the Rebbe used the term loosely here to mean that Zalman and Yosef, still young students, could have entered with their family into the audience, although they felt that they were unprepared. The Rebbe's words were relayed to them and taken to heart.

Out of Town

When he completed his studies at the Lubavitch Yeshivah in Brooklyn, Zalman decided to go to the yeshiva in Montreal, Canada. Many great Chabad Chassidim were living in the city then. He spent hours listening to their stories and sayings. He watched Reb Peretz Mochkin carefully and emulated his fervor for divine service. He also learned several lesser-known *nigunim* from the older Chassidim (some of which he recorded and can be listened to at ZalmanDeitsch.com).

Since there was no room in the dormitory, Rabbi Friedman and Zalman stayed at the home of an elderly man in the community. While they both enjoyed the man's attention and the stories he would tell, Rabbi Friedman later learned that "Zalman was also taking care of all of the man's needs, his papers, his legal matters, and his finances. He was a teenager, yet he devoted himself to taking care of this sweet old man," without being asked to, and without fanfare.

When a student was having trouble at the yeshiva, Zalman spent hours with him, guiding him and forever changing his life. Despite all this, Zalman "never missed any time of learning" that he had committed himself to.

Rabbi Friedman called his time with Zalman in Montreal some of the best years of his life. "There were from his friends that were brighter than him," he said. "They knew much more than him, had a deeper understanding, had all sorts of talents, all sorts of abilities that were really impressive." Yet, somehow, Zalman made them feel humble.

He recalled farbrengens at the yeshiva: "We would have some fun. Everyone would show off a little bit, you know, cute expressions and brilliant criticisms and insights." Then the young men would glance over at Zalman, who was sitting there, obviously perplexed at their petty conversation, Rabbi Friedman said, and

The Rebbe encouraging the singing at a farbrengen, mid-1960s.

"We would get serious. We would tell ourselves, 'Let's get sober.'"

Zalman told many stories about his time in Montreal. He spoke with great affection about his mashpia Rabbi Pinchus Korf, a member of the yeshiva's faculty. For example, at one farbrengen Rabbi Korf told the bochurim that there was a couple in the community, Rabbi Leibel and Sara Raizel Wolowik, who were married for three years but were not blessed with children. "This is an auspicious time to give them a *berachah*, for it is known that what a farbrengen can do, not even Malach Michoel can do, and we should all answer *amen*," he said. The couple had their first child the next year.

After their first year in the yeshiva, Zalman and his friends wanted to return to New York, but the Rebbe told them to remain in Montreal. Before Purim 5726 (1966), Zalman requested to go to New York to attend the Rebbe's farbrengen. Rabbi Korf declined to give him permission, however.

Early the next morning, seeing how much this meant to Zalman, Rabbi Korf came into his room. "Wake up and go," he told the stunned young man, giving him a plane ticket to New York. That Purim farbrengen was remembered as a special one in Chabad history. On this occasion the Rebbe announced, "Anyone who stretches out their hand, you give them," quoting from Jewish law that on Purim, one should give to anyone who asks for tzedakah.

Rabbi Pinchus Korf.

The Rebbe then stood for a long time, distributing l'chaim to all those who asked. Those present felt that they were also receiving blessings for everything they needed.

Sholom and Mirel took great pride in their son. Their dream of giving their children a true Chassidic education had finally come true. Sholom joked that Zalman studied so diligently that he rarely called home. When he finally did call, it was to inform them that he would be visiting New York the next day.

At the end of their second year, the group of students Zalman was with again asked the Rebbe's permission to study at 770. This time it was granted. There Zalman had a new study partner, Rabbi Leibel Kaplan, who later became the unforgettable director of Chabad in Tzfas, Israel.

Zalman was eventually designated one of the "*kanim* of Chassidus" (kanim refers to the seven branches of the menorah in the Beis Hamikdash). It was a title given to seven students who the Rebbe said should study additional hours after the regular schedule. Each member of the group would deliver a *pilpul*, scholarly talk, once every seven weeks, which would

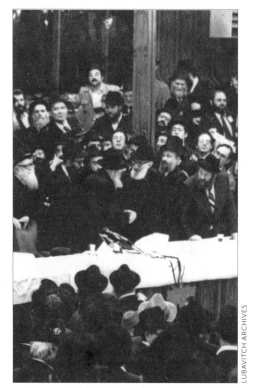

Rabbi Soloveitchik at the Rebbe's farbrengen, 1980.

later be printed and distributed.

The kanim would take turns walking directly behind the Rebbe when he went home on Friday nights, a privilege that Zalman treasured.

One night, Zalman came home visibly elated after delivering his pilpul in front of the other students. "Zalmanke, it looks like you feel like one of the elite," his father told him. Zalman understood the message. He should not let his success in his studies go to his head.

Farbrengen with Rabbi Soloveitchik

In 1969, a large event in honor of the 19th of Kislev was organized by Chabad in Boston. Rabbi Yosef Ber Soloveitchik was slated to speak. Seven students from 770, Zalman among them, were asked to attend. The students hoped that they would find an opportunity to discuss their studies with the great rabbi.

They sat in the audience as Rabbi Soloveitchik spoke about the founder of Chabad, Rabbi Schneur Zalman of Liadi, noting that he was originally from Lithuania, where the

"Jewish Peace Corps" Visitors

Zalman Deitsch (left) and Israel Shmotkin display materials they are distributing to Orthodox Jewish families this week. Rabbinical students at Lubavitcher Yeshiva in New York City, they are members of the "Jewish Peace Corps." The organization, founded in 1951, is to reawaken an awareness of Judaism among those of the Jewish faith.

Report in *The Evening Gazette*, Worcester, Massachusetts, 1967.

Jews were known for their opposition to Chassidism. Before he was about to go home, he turned to the students and said, "Today is Yud Tes Kislev, we need to *farbreng.*"

The students, along with some local Lubavitchers and a few of Rabbi Soloveitchik's own students, joined the spontenious gathering. The students and Rabbi Soloveitchik, recalled Rabbi Leibel Schapiro, one of the students in the group and today *rosh yeshiva* of Chabad's Yeshivah Gedolah Rabbinical College of Greater Miami, spent time discussing the Rebbe's teachings. "One of the things we discussed was the Rambam on the *halachos* of *teshuvah.*"

At one point, Zalman would say, Rabbi Soloveitchik described how, when his wife passed away, the Rebbe sent a delegation of older Chassidim to be *menachem avel*. With tears in his eyes, he told them, "I immediately knew that only someone who learns Chassidus has the capability to understand my pain."

The students submitted a report about the event and the farbrengen to the Rebbe. The Rebbe thanked them and blessed them with success in their studies, adding that he hoped they had shared some of their own original Torah insights, in addition to "what the Rebbe said at farbrengens."

Zalman repeated the story about Rabbi Soloveitchik at a Chassidic gathering years later in Springfield, Massachusetts. "Rabbi Soloveitchik's expression of the importance of learning Chassidus impressed me more than what I heard from many Chassidim over the years," he concluded.

Rabbi Yehoshua Botnick, who was present at the Springfield farbrengen, said that the story "changed my life." He transferred to a yeshiva where he could study Chassidus and later became the director of Chabad of the Carleton Region in Ottawa, ON.

Service of the Heart

In one of Zalman's private audiences with the Rebbe, he received a directive that he would take seriously his entire life. The Rebbe told him to pray at length, with intention and contemplation, a practice known among Chassidim as *davening b'avodah*.

The Chassid prepares for davening and contemplates the greatness of Hashem. They meditate that their purpose in life is to serve Hashem and that He recreates our world from nothing every moment. Many times a stirring nigun departs the Chassid's lips as they think about each word of the davening.

As a young student, Zalman would leave the house early in the morning in order to study Chassidus before davening. The sound of the door closing behind him was her alarm clock, Mirel said later, and a joyful reminder that her son was following in the footsteps of great Chassidim.

After his marriage, Zalman still awoke at 6 a.m. each morning to study, though he could not spend as much time davening as he had as a young man. Shabbos became his sacred time. "I am careful to daven every day with a *minyan*, and on Shabbos, as the Rebbe told me, to daven b'avodah," he once told his daughter. When she recalled this story later, she said, "I feel bad now that as children we would knock on the shul door at around two o'clock to tell him that we were waiting for him to make Kiddush and eat the Shabbos meal."

One day in the early 1980s, a freight train carrying merchandise Zalman had ordered was delayed, not an uncommon occurrence. That day, however, it was especially frustrating.

It was the eve of Yom Kippur. While the community in Crown Heights was busy immersing in the mikvah, eating festive meals, and preparing for the holiest day of the year, Zalman and his brother Yosef were stuck at a dangerous freight train depot in New Jersey, waiting with a tractor-trailer to pick up a large delivery of fabrics.

Anxiety levels climbed as the train tarried, and they wondered if it would arrive before the holiday started. It did, but by the time the truck had delivered the merchandise to the warehouse, it was very late. Tired and frazzled, Zalman made it home just in time to grab a bite to eat, bless his children, and stop at the mikvah on the way to 770.

Avraham Moshe recalled seeing him at shul for the Kol Nidrei prayers that usher in the holiday. "Knowing what happened that day, I was expecting him to go home after davening that night to rest. Yet he stayed, said Tehillim, and learned a maamar, as he would do every year. For those who witnessed it, this made a great impression."

Zalman (fourth from left) during kos shel berachah with the Rebbe.

Expression of Love

Chassidim established the custom of giving *maamad*, a regular donation to the Rebbe, which the Rebbe would use for his personal needs and for his communal activities. The term is derived from the Hebrew word meaning "base" or "foundation," and the Chassidim would say that this regular donation to the Rebbe was a spiritual foundation upon which the rest of their divine service rested. It was a way to connect to the Rebbe in a practical way and, by relinquishing some of their physical sustenance, to demonstrate self-sacrifice.

When he was still a student at 770, Zalman began giving maamad, twenty dollars, to the Rebbe every month. It was a large amount for a student at the time, and raised some eyebrows, but Zalman never saw the problem. "I love the Rebbe, and this money is for the Rebbe," he said.

THE FOUR CUPS

I t was Achron Shel Pesach 1966. Avrohom Moshe Deitsch, then eleven years old, accompanied his father to the Rebbe's farbrengen. Although the yom tov would end in a few hours, the Rebbe discussed matzah, the Exodus from Egypt, and the theme of the day, the coming of Moshiach. "Pesach is one long yom tov," the Rebbe explained. "During the first two days, we celebrate the redemption of the *Yidden* from Egypt; today is dedicated to the future Redemption."

Everyone partook in "Moshiach's *seuda*" by eating matzah and drinking four cups of wine. While the Chassidim sang nigunim, the Rebbe looked around and acknowledged those who raised their cups to toast him with a l'chaim. At one point, the Rebbe motioned in Sholom's direction. Sholom did nothing, assuming the Rebbe meant someone else. The Rebbe kept repeating the motion, however, and eventually Sholom raised his cup to toast the Rebbe.

The Rebbe encourages someone to say l'chaim at a farbrengen, 1960.

The Rebbe acknowledged him but continued to point in his direction, and Sholom soon realized that the Rebbe was pointing to Avrohom Moshe, who was sitting behind him on the table. A cup of wine was immediately brought, which the young boy drank. After the next talk, during the singing, the Rebbe motioned again to Avrohom Moshe with three fingers, and Avrohom Moshe drank another cup of wine. After the third and fourth talks, the Rebbe motioned, first with two fingers, and then with one, indicating that he should drink the last of the four cups.

Sholom was perplexed. It was highly unusual for the Rebbe to tell young children to drink wine at all, let alone four full cups.

After the farbrengen, the Rebbe led the *bentching*, and following maariv, made Havdalah over the same cup of wine. Then he distributed wine from the cup for *"kos shel berachah"* ("the cup of blessing," i.e., the cup over which the blessing had been recited).

When it was Sholom's turn to receive some wine, the Rebbe motioned with his hand in wonder, as if to say, "Where is the boy?"

Sholom explained that, after drinking all that wine, he had been taken home by a neighbor and went straight to bed. The Rebbe responded with a big smile.

Six Weeks Later . . .

That Shavuos, Sholom had chest pains. He was immediately rushed to the hospital, where the doctors said he was undergoing a heart attack—his situation was critical. His two older children, Zalman and

Sholom with Avrohom Moshe.

Yosef, decided to go to 770 to ask the Rebbe for a berachah.

When they arrived, the Rebbe was in the middle of the yom tov meal upstairs in the apartment of the Previous Rebbe, where the Rebbe ate the yom tov meals until the passing of Rebbetzin Nechamah Dinah, the Previous Rebbe's wife, in 5731 (1971). The two approached the table and in a few words described the situation. The Rebbe gave them a piece of challah from the table and said, "This should be for healing."

During that Shavuos farbrengen, Sholom's place was empty. Afterward, Zalman and Yosef got on line to receive wine from the Rebbe's cup and ask for another blessing for their father.

After a long hospital stay, Sholom was finally stable enough to return home. He wrote to the Rebbe about his situation, requesting another blessing for a complete recovery. The Rebbe's response surprised him: "I already gave your son four cups as a blessing!"

Sholom began visiting heart specialists as far away as Boston. During this time, he scheduled a private audience with

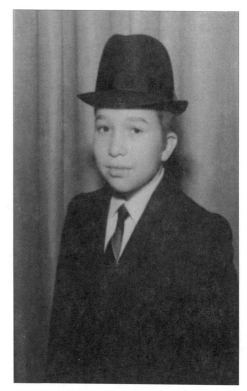

Avrohom Moshe at his bar mitzvah.

the Rebbe, intending to ask for a blessing for his health. When he entered the Rebbe's study, however, he suddenly felt ashamed to ask for his own personal needs. "I came to ask a blessing that the Rebbe should be healthy," he said instead. *"Az ich vet heren besurois toivois, vel ich zein gezunt,"* the Rebbe responded. When I will hear good news from Chassidim, I will be healthy.

With the Rebbe's blessings, Sholom survived, though he never resumed his former work schedule. Over the next few years, he had additional heart complications, making work very difficult, and on occasion, Zalman reluctantly took some time from his studies to help his father with the business.

Sholom and Mirel in their Crown Heights home, 1963.

"With Greater Vigor"

In honor of their anniversary, which was a few days after Sukkos, Sholom and Mirel hosted a grand farbrengen on Shemini Atzeres every year, celebrating their personal triumph over Communism, a victory that now manifested itself in their proud, observant children. Hundreds of guests would come during the course of the night to enjoy the food and the Chassidic atmosphere. They would prepare food in great quantities and alcoholic beverages. "Everyone remembers these yearly affairs, even today," Mirel wrote.

At a farbrengen on *Parshas Shemini*, 1963, the Rebbe announced that Chassidim under the age of forty should have no more than three small glasses of *mashke* at a time (in later years, it became four). Just before Shavuos of 1968, he made it known that this was his personal regulation (*Toras Menachem*, vol. 52, p. 414):

"Everyone has free choice to do the opposite of my request," the Rebbe said to the organizers of the *tahalucha*, the initiative of walking to shuls outside of Crown Heights to share words of

Chassidus and bring extra joy to other congregations on the holiday. "When it comes to participating in the tahalucha on Shavuos, which is my initiative, I ask and let it be known that those who did not follow it [the restriction on excessive drinking] are not my representatives, and I ask them not to join the tahalucha." The Rebbe added that this requirement would apply to his other initiatives.

At the farbrengen on the second day of Shavuos the Rebbe praised all those who had complied with his request and gone on tahalucha (ibid., vol. 53, p. 36), "It was enough to speak about this, with all of the tumult, before yom tov."

These were strong words, and even those who might have been more liberal during joyous holidays like Shemini Atzeres began to restrict themselves then as well. Sholom was in a dilemma. He worried that people would avoid their gathering that year. He told the Rebbe in a yechidus during the month before Tishrei, "I cannot just serve water and juice. What will be with my kiddush?"

The Rebbe responded, "*Bei dir in sukkah zolst machen be'yeser sees u'be'yeser oiz*" (In your sukkah, you should make [the kiddush] even bigger and with greater vigor). It was said that the celebration that year was the largest ever. "It seemed as if the whole of Lubavitch had come to celebrate at our sukkah," Mirel wrote. "The walls of our sukkah finally succumbed."

MASS. PIONEERS

One Shabbos in 1969, along with many other guests, a young woman from Massachusetts joined the Deitsches' table. Cyrel Edelman was a student at Beth Rivkah Seminary and worked after hours at the school. With her keen perception of people, she saw immediately that the family's kindness was outstanding.

Cyrel herself had been brought up in a home where hospitality was paramount. Her parents, Rabbi Dovid and Rebbetzin Leah Edelman, shluchim in Springfield, Massachusetts, for more than six decades, were pioneers of the Chabad movement in the United States.

Dovid was the son of Yechezkel Meir and Tobah Leah Edelman. He was raised in Baltimore, Maryland, in a religious home, but did not know anything about the Chassidic way of life. His first exposure to Chabad was in March 1940, at the age of fifteen, when

Rabbi Dovid and Leah Edelman.

he came across a newspaper report about the Previous Rebbe's arrival to the United States. The photograph of the Rebbe had a strong effect on him, and he cut it out and pasted it on the wall near his bed.

Later that year, Dovid became acquainted with the venerable Chassid Rabbi Avraham Eliyahu Akselrod. Rabbi Akselrod once said that to live a religious life in America, one has to have "sacks of self-sacrifice." He would regularly give classes in Chassidus in Baltimore's Tzemach Tzedek Shul, where he was the rabbi. Dovid began attending the classes and developed a deep appreciation for the teachings.

In 1941, he travelled to New York to study at Yeshiva Torah Vodaas, then in the Williamsburg neighborhood of Brooklyn, although Rabbi Akselrod had encouraged him to join the newly founded Tomchei Temimim Lubavitch Yeshivah.

Curious, in late spring of that year, Dovid went to visit 770. There he met young men who had a special zest for Torah and for life. They impressed him with their knowledge, not only of Gemara, but of Chassidus. After Shavuos that year, without waiting for his high school graduation, he transferred to the Lubavitch Yeshivah, where he was in the proximity of the Previous Rebbe and was deeply influenced by him.

That summer, the Previous Rebbe's son-in-law and eventual successor, Rabbi Menachem M. Schneerson, arrived in America with his wife, Rebbetzin Chaya Mushka. "While the older students went to the pier, the younger ones, including myself, greeted them upon arrival in 770," Rabbi Edelman later recalled. "All day long Chassidim came to 'give *shalom*' to the Rebbe and the Rebbetzin. We asked the Rebbe to farbreng, and the Rebbe said that after he received an *aliyah* to the Torah on Thursday and 'bentched *gomel*,' he would make a farbrengen."

Rabbi Edelman remembered the farbrengen that was held to celebrate the couple's miraculous escape from Europe, adding that he had merited to attend the Rebbe's first farbrengen on the shores of the United States, the farbrengen when he accepted the mantle of leadership in 1951, as well as the last farbrengen, as of now, on Shabbos, the 25th of Adar in 1992.

Soon after the Previous Rebbe arrived in the United States, he saw that what the American Jewish communities needed most was day schools, and he began establishing Chabad schools in communities all over the East Coast where Jewish education was not available.

One Friday morning in 1943, when Rabbi Edelman had been in the Lubavitch Yeshivah for three years, the Previous Rebbe summoned him to his office and directed him to go to Bridgeport, Connecticut, to establish a school. Rabbi Edelman, then 19, asked if he should go before Shabbos. If possible, the Rebbe responded, yes.

Rabbi Edelman went back to the study hall, recruited another

The Previous Rebbe with his son-in-law and eventual successor, the Rebbe, 1942.

student to accompany him, and the two left for Bridgeport that day. Two more rabbinical students would later join them there.

Nine months later, the Previous Rebbe instructed Rabbi Edelman to leave Bridgeport and go to Pittsburgh, Pennsylvania, to help Rabbi Sholom Posner run the school and, as he said, "to bring the spirit of Chassidus [there]."

A year later, he was sent to Buffalo, New York, where he remained for three years, during which the school there became very successful. Throughout, the Previous Rebbe gave him detailed guidance on how the schools should be run.

At one point, he wrote to the Previous Rebbe asking permission to return to his studies at 770. The Rebbe replied that he should be happy in the merit of his sacred mission, adding that his Torah studies in his current location would be more successful than in Brooklyn, "For when you help others spiritually, your mind and heart become a thousandfold more refined" (see *Torah Ohr* 1b).

Rabbi Yisroel and Rebbetzin Zlata Zuber.

In the spring of 1948, Rabbi Edelman married Leah Zuber. Leah was no stranger to sacred missions. Her parents served as Chabad representatives in far-off cities such as Sachkhere, Georgia, and Stockholm, Sweden.

In Stockholm, where Rabbi Yaakov Yisroel Zuber served as the leader of the Jewish community in the roles of chief rabbi, *shochet*, and mohel from 1930 to 1947, the Zubers were one of two Chabad families, yet they maintained a strong Chassidic home and raised their children to be proud of their heritage. In the 1940s, Leah watched as her parents assisted refugees of World War II and later, survivors of the Holocaust. Notably, the family tended to the needs of the Previous Rebbe and his entourage during their stopover in Sweden on the way to America in 1940.

With the Previous Rebbe's blessings, the Zubers moved to Boston in 1947. Rabbi Zuber was first the director of the local Chabad day school, then the rabbi at the Chabad shul, and later the assistant rabbi at Congregation Beth Hamidrash Hagodol in Roxbury, where he was adored for his scholarship and his dedication to the community.

After their wedding, the Edelmans moved to Boston, where the rabbi taught for half the day at the Chabad school and was rabbi at a Young Israel shul. He also hosted a Sunday program on Jewish topics at a local radio station.

Then, in late 1949, Rabbi Edelman, then twenty-four, received a phone call from Rabbi Sh-

Rabbis Zuber and Edelman during an outdoor learning session, circa 1947.

maryahu Gurary, the Previous Rebbe's son-in-law. The Rashag, as he was known, told him to take the reins of the Chabad day school in Springfield, Massachusetts. The couple was expecting their second child, and Rabbi Edelman stayed in Springfield during the week, while his wife lived with her family. After their daughter Cyrel was born, Rebbetzin Edelman joined him in Springfield.

Together with two other young men, whom he recruited from the Lubavitch Yeshivah in Brooklyn, Rabbi Edelman expanded the day school, adding a day camp, children's clubs, adult-education classes, and all the other activities associated with a Chabad House today. They also took the initiative to reach out to Jews in

Zalman and Cyrel's engagement celebration. From left: Rabbi
Dovid Edelman, Zalman, Rabbi Nosson Noteh Zuber, and Dovid Deitsch.

neighboring towns and cities, many of which eventually received
their own shluchim.

The Edelmans' work in Springfield was not easy, requiring
much self-sacrifice and Chassidic determination. Many families
in the area attribute their Jewish identity and observance to their
efforts. Cyrel always planned to follow in her parents' footsteps,
certain that her future husband would join the Rebbe's army of
shluchim by bringing Yiddishkeit to a community where it was
lacking.

The Proposal

In the winter of 1969, Zalman's name was suggested to Cyrel Edelman as a potential match. "The first time I met Zalman, I saw in
front of me a young, bashful man," recalled Cyrel's mother, Rebbetzin Edelman. After spending some time with the young man,
she said, she saw much more than that. "Zalman turned out to
be someone with a good heart, well-mannered, and intelligent. I

Artist Hendel Lieberman, the Deitsches' cousin,
leads the singing of nigunim at the engagement celebration.

Reb Bentche Shemtov leading a farbrengen at the engagement celebration. Sitting left
is Rabbi Manis Friedman. In the back row are (left to right) Rabbi Itche Gurevitch, Rabbi
Yerachmiel Stillman, and Avrohom Moshe.

Zalman and Cyrel with their parents, Rabbi Dovid and
Rebbetzin Leah Edelman (left) and Sholom and Mirel Deitsch.

noticed how he gave his undivided attention to the other person.
I was quickly impressed by him and felt that it would be a great
merit for us for Zalman to be a part of our family. We gave our
blessing to the match."

Before finalizing their engagement, Zalman and Cyrel wrote
to the Rebbe, asking for his blessing. "The match is a good idea,"
the Rebbe responded; the engagement "should be in a good time
and with success in everything." They became engaged on the 21st
of Adar (March 11th) 1969.

The Shabbos after the engagement, Sholom walked over to the
Rebbe's table during the farbrengen and, sincere in the belief that
the Rebbe had played a critical role in the match, said, "I want to
thank the Rebbe for the *shidduch*."

"For matchmaking you have to pay," the Rebbe responded
with a smile, without specifying what the payment would be. Sholom never had the opportunity to ask.

IN MIDDLE OF THE NIGHT

As the wedding neared, the family found more reason to rejoice. Their father's health seemed to be improving. "My father, may he be well, Sholom Yeshaya ben Hinda, is in general, thank G-d, feeling good," Zalman wrote to the Rebbe at the time. Everyone hoped that Sholom would fully return to himself.

A month and a half later, in the middle of the night of the 5th of Iyar, Sholom suffered another heart attack. The family called an ambulance, but when the paramedics arrived, they said there was nothing they could do.

Zalman immediately called the Rebbe's office; Rabbi Chaim Mordechai Aizik Hodakov, the Rebbe's chief aide, answered the phone. When he heard what had happened, he said that he could not call the Rebbe's house directly at that hour, but if they felt it was urgent, they should call. "Don't worry, the Rebbe is up now," he said when Zalman seemed hesitant, and provided Zalman with the phone number.

Feeling that the situation required extreme measures, Zalman called the Rebbe's home. He recalled waiting while the phone rang twice, though it seemed like an eternity, when Rebbetzin Chaya Mushka answered. After apologizing profusely, Zalman told her what had happened and asked if she could relay the information to the Rebbe.

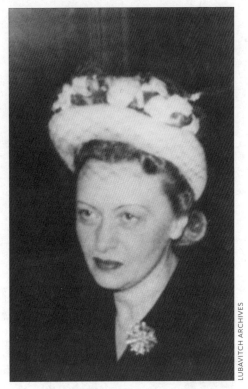

Rebbetzin Chaya Mushka.

The Rebbetzin asked him to stay on the line. She returned to the phone and said, "My husband asked that they should still take him to the hospital and that they should call from there to report on the situation."

Sholom was rushed to the hospital, where he was pronounced deceased by the doctors. He was a month away from his fifty-first birthday. Zalman called the Rebbe's home again to report the news. The Rebbetzin answered immediately this time. She relayed the Rebbe's response to Zalman, "They should keep an eye on their mother."

Many people participated in the funeral, including the Rebbe,

Zalman and Avrohom Moshe.

who joined the procession as it passed 770. During *minchah* that day, the Chassidim saw tears rolling down the Rebbe's face.

The family noted that the entry in *Hayom Yom* for the 5th of Iyar is very befitting:

> The Alter Rebbe received the following teaching from the saintly R. Mordechai, who heard it from the Baal Shem Tov: "A soul descends into this world and lives seventy or eighty years in order to do a Jew a material favor, and certainly a spiritual one."

Some time after Sholom's passing, the family asked the Rebbe's forgiveness for having bothered him at such a late hour. "For someone like Sholom," the Rebbe responded, "time is of no matter."

Reflecting on that time, Mirel recalled the special anniversary celebration, which the Rebbe had encouraged earlier that year. "[It] was to be the last kiddush Sholom and I made together." She would continue to host a gathering on that day until the end of her life.

"Sholom and I had twenty-three happy and loving years together," she concluded. "Hashem took my Sholom, and a part of me died with him."

A Different Course

The Deitsch family was suddenly thrown into unknown territory, grieving for their beloved father and breadwinner while preparing for a wedding. Every day brought new pain and new challenges. As the oldest child, it took all of Zalman's strength to pull the family through.

As was the custom, before the wedding the whole family went for a private audience to receive the Rebbe's blessing. After the Rebbe had showered them with blessings, Mirel reminded the Rebbe of his comment that one should pay for matchmaking. "What sort of payment did the Rebbe have in mind?" she asked.

The Rebbe said that she should be besimchah, joyous. "This is the fee that I am asking for." When she asked how it was possible for her at this time to be joyous, the Rebbe responded, "If you strengthen your bitachon [trust] in Hashem, then you will be besimchah."

The Rebbe then turned to Mirel and all the family members present and said, "I am asking of you to please strengthen your belief and faith in the Creator of the world." Then Mirel asked a question that had clearly been weighing on her: "Rebbe, how can I stand under the chuppah without my husband and not break down in tears?"

"You will not cry under the *chuppah*," the Rebbe said. But Mirel wasn't satisfied. "How can I be joyous when my husband passed away, leaving me alone with four children still to raise?"

"Surely it will be good," the Rebbe responded, reiterating that when she would strengthen her trust in Hashem, it would bring

Sholom and Mirel, 1968.

Mirel with the Rebbe, 1991. Her son Yosef is in the center.

joy.

Mirel then asked who would support her family, to which the Rebbe responded that Zalman would take over his father's textile business and help support his mother and siblings. "But he doesn't have any experience," Mirel said. The Rebbe lifted his holy hand, smiled, and said, "He will yet learn." He blessed them that the business should prosper, with the same words he had used with Sholom several years earlier about their Sukkos farbrengen, *"be'yeser se'es u'be'yeser oiz"* (even more vigorously).

In the later years, at every *sheva berachos* in the Deitsch family, Zalman would recount how the Rebbe told his father that one has to pay for a shidduch, and the fee the Rebbe had requested of his mother. "Although someone else may be occupied with the actual matchmaking," he would say, "you clearly see that the Rebbe agreed with my father, that ultimately the Rebbe is the matchmaker."

He would add that one always has to pay the Rebbe's "fee."

"Every person needs to ask what fee the Rebbe wants of them," he said. "From Bubby, the Rebbe wanted more trust that would bring more joy. From each of us it may be something else."

Part IV

The Businessman

TEXTILE BEGINNINGS

Zalman and Cyrel celebrated their marriage on the 21st of Elul 5729 (September 4, 1969). As the Rebbe had assured her, Mirel did not cry under the chuppah. Hundreds came to celebrate, wish the entire Deitsch family well, share in the simchah, and bring the new couple much joy.

They settled into a modest apartment on the third floor of 701 Empire Boulevard in Crown Heights. There was little time for leisure or celebration, however. Though they had anticipated leaving Crown Heights as shluchim in the Rebbe's army, based on the Rebbe's directive, they now understood that their mission lay closer to home. The financial responsibility of the family lay squarely on Zalman's shoulders, and after the wedding he entered the world of commerce.

He also began *kollel*, a full-time program of Torah study for

Zalman on the way to the chuppah.

newly married men, and continued to lead the davening three times a day with a minyan in order to say Kaddish for his father. In a letter to the Rebbe, he asked how to balance all these responsibilities, and the Rebbe directed him to learn only half a day in kollel and work half a day. He followed this regimen for close to two years.

The first steps in the textile business were not easy. Competition was fierce, and no allowances were made for beginners. More than once he asked himself, "What am I doing here?" But he never forgot the Rebbe's words in that fateful private audience, "He will yet learn," and the blessing that the business should prosper *"be'yeser sees u'be'yeser oiz."* He knew he was not alone—he had the Rebbe's berachah with him.

The office of Deitsch Textile, which Zalman shared with his mother, was a cramped room in a New Jersey warehouse where hundreds of rolls of fabric in various materials and designs were waiting to be measured, cut, and shipped off to customers.

Studying at the kitchen table.

In yeshiva, Zalman had been a stellar student whose world was contained within the volumes of Chassidus and Gemara. His heart had never been in measuring tape and rolls of fabric.

Now, as he entered the warehouse each morning, he yearned to be back in yeshiva, tackling a difficult piece of Gemara or Chassidic discourse, chanting the singsong of a maamar, mapping the Creation of the world as explained in Chassidic teachings.

If he could not be in kollel, at least he could ensure that his business had a soul. He would be scrupulously honest, he resolved, and use his profits to partner with the Rebbe's shluchim. Thus he would combine the worlds of business and shlichus.

Zalman's approach to business brings to mind the famed Chassid of the Alter Rebbe, Reb Binyomin Kletzker. Reb Binyomin was once calculating the profits from his lumber business, and at the bottom of a long column of figures wrote the words, "*Ein od milvado*" (There is none besides Hashem). When someone asked how he could mix business and Chassidus, he responded,

"It happens that during davening to the Master of the Universe, a person's mind sometimes wanders to the world of business. Why, then, should we wonder if our minds wander to G-d in the midst of business dealings?" (*Toras Menachem*, vol. 7, p. 56).

While his mother dealt with the paperwork and bookkeeping, Zalman did the purchasing and sales. Under his leadership, the business grew and prospered, just as the Rebbe had predicted.

BUSINESS MODEL

Zalman absorbed much of his business ethos from his uncle Reb Dovid Deitsch, who ran Deitsch Plastic Co., a successful vinyl business based in New Haven, Connecticut. A soft-spoken, charismatic man, Reb Dovid was a devoted Chabad Chassid: modest, kind, and extremely charitable. He contributed to many organizations and was among the founders of the Educational Institute Oholei Torah, today one of the largest Chabad yeshivas, with some 1,850 students. To this day, he and his wife are affectionately known as the "father and mother of Oholei Torah." Zalman would speak admiringly about his uncle, who was a Chassid first and a businessman second.

An extraordinary story lay behind Reb Dovid's success. At a farbrengen on the 19th of Kislev 5718 (1957), the Rebbe raised funds for new housing in Kfar Chabad. He emphasized the importance of the project, saying, "Surely all those gathered here will

The Rebbe and Dovid Deitsch.

give—in large and befitting amounts—according to their hearts' desires."

Then, to everyone's surprise, the Rebbe stated that he reserved the right to change the amounts people had pledged. "In general, I do not become involved in the amount of every individual's donation. I am either content [with it] or I am not, in which case I keep it to myself. However, since this cause is an exception to the rule, I am changing my usual practice. If I see that someone is giving too little, I will not be shy to instruct him—authorized by the urgency of the cause [the new housing]—to increase the pledge as I see fit."

The Rebbe then promised that Hashem would reimburse each donor at least four times the amount of his pledge. This extraordinary statement and the opportunity it presented were not lost on those present. The attendees took cards, wrote down their pledges, and passed them to the Rebbe, who immediately looked at them.

Looking at Reb Sholom Deitsch's card, the Rebbe called out, "Sholom Deitsch, five times that amount!" His brother Reb Dovid wrote down $3,000. When the Rebbe saw the amount, he called out, "Dovid Deitsch, ten times that amount!"

The businessman was shocked. He had already pledged a large sum, more than he thought he could currently give, yet as a Chassid he had faith that he would find a way to fulfill the pledge. The farbrengen ended at four in the morning, and Reb Dovid made his way back to New Haven, where he lived. Later that morning, he noticed his bank manager walking in the street. Mustering his courage, he approached, and with the air of someone making a routine request, asked for a $30,000 loan.

The banker looked at him as if he had fallen from the moon. "And why, Mr. Deitsch, do you think the bank would lend you such a large amount of money?" he asked.

Without blinking, Reb Dovid replied, "Place $10,000 against my home, $10,000 against my business, and another $10,000 on my word."

The bank manager knew Reb Dovid. Although he still had a mortgage on his home, and his business did not have that value, he was indisputably honest. He agreed to the loan.

Within a few days, Reb Dovid brought the $30,000 to the Rebbe and returned home with his blessings.

A few days later, he received a phone call from an executive at a vinyl company in Boston. "Dave, we had a big fire at our manufacturing site. We have a large amount of vinyl with minor damage. We want to begin renovating the warehouse and are willing to sell it at a reduced rate. Are you interested in a deal?"

At the time, Reb Dovid was buying much smaller amounts of vinyl than the company was offering, but seizing the opportunity to grow, he hired a truck to go to Boston. All the vinyl was soon sold at three times the normal profit.

The company called him again and offered more. This time Reb Dovid hired a larger truck, filled it up in Boston, and again sold the materials for a large profit. When he got a third call, he hired an even larger truck and emptied out the warehouse.

After all of the vinyl was sold and his original $30,000 donation to the Rebbe was recovered, he traveled to New York and wrote the Rebbe another check for $30,000. The Rebbe told his secretary to return it, however. "Tell him that if he agrees, I would like to be a partner in his business," the Rebbe said.

Sholom Deitsch (left) with his older brother Dovid.

LUBAVITCH ARCHIVES

"For a better partner, I could never have dreamed," Reb Dovid said. He left 770 delighted. From then on, his business continued to grow into a multimillion-dollar enterprise.

The lesson of his uncle's story was clear to Zalman: if he wanted to be a good businessman, he had to follow the Rebbe's directives and give a lot of tzedakah to the Rebbe and the Rebbe's organizations.

(A similar sentiment had been expressed by the Previous Rebbe, who wrote to someone who was ill that he should give tzedakah immediately, for "it is better that Hashem should owe the person, and He will of course repay, than that the person owe

Hashem money" [*Igros Kodesh*, vol. 7, p. 1].)

When Zalman started out in business, Reb Dovid provided advice and encouragement. Once, Zalman was visiting his uncle's office and watched him write out a large commission check to one of his salespeople. "Isn't it a waste to give so much money to a salesperson?" he asked.

His uncle chuckled. "On the contrary," he said, "I wish that the amount could be larger. The higher the commission, the higher the sales. The higher the sales, the more we can give to tzedakah."

In his usual good-natured manner, he dispensed another piece of valuable advice: "In general, when you treat your workers properly, they repay you with more effort."

Zalman used to say that not only did he take the lesson to heart in the operation of his business, but he also applied it to his relationship with the Rebbe. Surely, for a good "worker," the Rebbe would give a large "commission." "Everything we do, the goal is to give the Rebbe nachas," he concluded.

Grandfather's Influence

Another influence on Zalman was his grandfather Reb Mendel Deitsch, whose dedication to tzedakah was legendary.

When Reb Mendel lived in Crown Heights, he once asked his son Dovid to come visit him. When he arrived from New Haven, his father told him, "Dovid, I invited you here because I need money."

Reb Dovid was taken aback. He thought that his father had all that he needed. He immediately took out his wallet and gave his father a large sum.

"Are you not embarrassed?" Reb Mendel admonished his son. "Your elderly father asks you for money, and this is all you have given him?"

Reb Dovid immediately took out more money from his wallet,

Mendel and Hinda Deitsch.

doubling the amount he had already given. With this, his father was pleased. "Very good!" he said. "Now be so good as to take this money to 770. Half of the money give to the Rebbe [for maamad], and the other half give to Merkos L'Inyonei Chinuch," the educational arm of the Chabad-Lubavitch movement.

Once, Reb Mendel learned that a close friend had opened a savings account. At first, Reb Mendel refused to even say hello to him. "How can one open a savings account when there are people who are in need?" he asked.

Proud Brothers

From his father, Zalman learned to respect his siblings. Reserved by nature, his uncle Reb Dovid would sit at the head table at Oholei Torah dinners to show his support for the institution and encourage others to do likewise. Zalman used to describe how his

Zalman with his brothers Yosef (center), and Avrohom Moshe.

father, Reb Sholom, would stand up and applaud his brother with the rest of the crowd. When Zalman's younger brother Yosef was the guest of honor at the Kollel Tiferes Zkeinim Levi Yitzchak dinner, he proudly did the same.

TOIL AND
BLESSINGS

I n the beginning of his business career, Zalman took bold steps. He purchased a large warehouse in Jersey City, New Jersey, and took out several loans. For the first few years, however, the business did not turn much of a profit.

"The business is now from the merchandise that we received from my uncle Dovid," he reported three years later to the Rebbe in Cheshvan 5733 (October 1972), as well as "with a little from the business my father started. *Baruch Hashem*, we are relatively successful." He concluded, "I am asking for the Rebbe's blessing that there should be immediate success, and that I should be able to give a lot of tzedakah."

After several years, with a gift for negotiating and a lot of very hard work, he began to purchase and sell textiles successfully.

Like his uncle, Zalman was naturally a quiet person, but he learned to speak his mind and run the business with resolve, refusing to let associates push him into deals he wasn't comfortable with.

At the time, suppliers preferred to sell to established companies with whom they had long-running relationships. Nevertheless, Zalman did not give up, continuously calling the companies and requesting to make orders. When that failed, he would travel to their offices and refuse to leave without a truckload of goods. He maintained good relations with these suppliers for many years, staving off competitors.

Rabbi Shaya Deitsch, the Chabad representative in Fort Washington, Pennsylvania, once confided to his father that he found fundraising challenging. "At first, my greatest difficulty in business was collecting debts from customers," Zalman told him. Knowing that this task was essential to the survival of his business, however, he made a point of doing it first thing each day before moving on to less trying duties.

The Rebbe's Guidance

From the very beginning, Zalman turned to the Rebbe to guide him in every detail in life, including his business decisions. Even after he found his footing and the business grew, he continued the practice he had begun in the early days of writing regular reports to the Rebbe about how the business was faring. He kept drafts of every one of those reports in his files with notes detailing the Rebbe's responses.

In 5732 (1972), at the age of twenty-five, he wrote to the Rebbe that he was considering purchasing a 25,000-square-foot warehouse. He added that his uncles, Dovid Deitsch and Mordechai Rivkin, thought it was a good idea. He asked for the Rebbe's approval and blessing.

If the two uncles agree to the above, the Rebbe responded, "with their advice, etc., you should look into the offer." He would

Receiving kos shel berachah from the Rebbe.

mention the matter at the *tziyun* (the resting place of the Previous Rebbe), the Rebbe wrote. He also wrote the word "Chitas," implying that Zalman's completion of the daily study regimen would contribute to the success of the venture.

In a follow-up letter, Zalman detailed all of the seller's conditions. "If the price is right," the Rebbe wrote back, the above is a worthwhile deal.

In the summer of that year, Zalman reported, in another letter to the Rebbe, that he was considering expanding the business into retail. "It is a good idea if it is not a contradiction in sales, since sometimes the wholesale buyers object [to the opening of retail locations]," the Rebbe responded.

Over the years the business expanded rapidly. The warehouse in Jersey City had become too small, and Zalman was considering purchasing a larger building. In 5736 (1975), he found a promising building in Brooklyn. "I spoke to the neighbors and to the local police station, and they said that it is a safe area, and especially

The Rebbe's participation toward the purchase of the warehouse at 372 Broadway, 1985.

the building we want to purchase is in a quiet part of that neighborhood," he wrote to the Rebbe, asking if it was a good idea to purchase the building or to look elsewhere.

The Rebbe placed a line through the words *if* and *to look elsewhere*, and made an arrow to *purchase the building,* adding, "If the neighborhood is fitting, you should take interest in the deal."

With the Rebbe's blessing, Zalman purchased the building at Washington and Atlantic Avenues in Brooklyn and turned it into a warehouse. He kept the Jersey City warehouse, which became a lucrative investment when the real estate was later in demand.

One theme that emerges from the Rebbe's advice to Zalman is not to make important decisions too quickly. Again and again, the Rebbe advised him to check and ensure that the decision made good business sense before proceeding.

At one point, Zalman was considering expanding the business into international markets. He wrote to the Rebbe that he had the opportunity to travel to West Africa and sell directly to the large wholesalers there.

The Rebbe gave his approval and blessing for the trip, but warned him to be careful about cutting out the middlemen. "It is a good idea to visit there. There is need for much deliberation to see if it is worth it to suspend [the middlemen]. [Please find] the attached [money] for [your trip], etc.," as a symbolic participation in the trip.

The Rebbe also gave a green light to a trip to Nigeria, which proved very profitable. When Zalman returned and reported that he felt there were more opportunities there, the Rebbe wrote, "It should be with great success." South America and Japan were next, and the Rebbe gave his blessing, promising to mention the trips at the Previous Rebbe's tziyun.

At one point, one of Zalman's connections in Nigeria took advantage of him and walked off with the goods without paying. It was a great loss, but Zalman took it as a sign from G-d and cut off all business in the country. A few years later, on December 31, 1983, the Nigerian military coup rendered all the assets invested in the country worthless.

Tragic Fire

On Sukkos 5740 (October 1979), at 3:30 in the afternoon, a large blaze engulfed the Deitsch Textile warehouse in Brooklyn. The fire was so fierce that the one hundred and fifty firemen who responded could not enter the building. While everyone on the first floor was evacuated, tragically, there was one casualty.

Though the cause of the fire remains a mystery until this day, almost immediately, the authorities blamed Zalman, his brother Yosef, and the building manager. They were taken to the police station for questioning.

"At 6 p.m., Chief Cruthers said the building was a total loss and in danger of collapsing," reported *The New York Times*. "He ordered firemen away to prevent injury. Late last night, the fear of collapse grew, according to fire officials, who said water poured on the fire was being soaked up by bales of fabric, increasing the weight on floors already weakened by the intense heat."

The fire wiped out the entire Deitsch family's livelihood, but

Zalman was also worried about his workers. He reported the fire to the Rebbe, who responded, "It should be the will of Hashem that the well-known statement of the exalted holy sages should be fulfilled.[1] You should report good news."

Four days later, as the smoldering warehouse continued to burn, the Deitsches were in Crown Heights, celebrating Simchas Torah, one of the most joyous days on the Jewish calendar.

At the Simchas Torah farbrengen (*Sichos Kodesh* 5740, vol. 1, p. 182), the Rebbe related how someone had once told the Previous Rebbe that he wanted to donate to Chabad's work of spreading Judaism at a level that was "more than his means." The Previous Rebbe responded that when someone makes an earnest decision to give more tzedakah than they can afford, Hashem opens new channels "so that it is possible to fulfill the pledge."

At the gathering, the Rebbe said that the man had not only made the large donation, but received a windfall himself. He paraphrased from the *passuk* (Bereishis 47:24) that just as the Israelites had been instructed to give "one-fifth to Pharaoh," which the *Zohar* says is a reference to Hashem, "and the other four parts for yourself," Hashem would repay fourfold the one who gave to others.

Since this story became known to us, the Rebbe said, it means that we should learn from it and follow this man's example, trusting G-d to open the channels. The Rebbe stipulated, however, that the decision to give should be made during the farbrengen.

Zalman had no idea how he would be able to make any donation, let alone a large sum, but he understood that if the Rebbe made the request, it was an auspicious time to pledge a large

---

1. The Tzemach Tzedek quotes the Alter Rebbe, who writes that he heard it from "the righteous," that when a person's property is burned (a sign of judgment), afterward, mercy and kindness come to the person (see *Derech Mitzvoisechah* 198b).

Doing business in Nigeria.

amount.

Immediately after Simchas Torah, he borrowed money, brought a large check to the Rebbe, and wrote simply, "In connection with the Rebbe's talk on this Simchas Torah," adding his name, his mother's, his family, and the family partners, "this is our first installment."

He soon received a call from Rabbi Leibel Groner, one of the Rebbe's secretaries, saying that the Rebbe wanted to know if the decision was made during the farbrengen and wholeheartedly. Zalman responded with certainty that it was. While the Rebbe did not accept several other people's donations made at the time, he did accept Zalman's.

Not long afterward, Zalman found a new warehouse, and with loans from various sources, he jumpstarted the business with a whole new warehouse of goods. After several years of legal battles, the courts ruled that there was no definite proof that the casualty was caused by the Deitsch brothers' negligence; the charges were dropped and they were vindicated, freeing them to grow the business.

Diversifying

In the 5740s (1980s), the textile market was in decline. Zalman realized he would need to diversify the business. He wrote to the Rebbe about branching out into real estate. In the fall of 5744 (1983), the Rebbe advised him to proceed on a particular deal, "according to the suggestions of knowledgeable friends (plural)."

A few days later, Zalman wrote again: "We have a chance now to purchase a large building with several partners, and I am asking for the Rebbe's blessing." The Rebbe gave his blessing, adding that he wanted to participate as well and was including a one hundred-dollar bill.

Around a year later, the Deitsch family sold the building for more than double the purchase price.

Despite his success, Zalman never lost sight of his goal. His bottom line was not financial profit, but the Rebbe's satisfaction and approval. As he concluded in one of his reports, "I am asking the Rebbe for much success in all of my business ventures, and I should merit to give the Rebbe *nachas ruach*."

Help from Above

Decades after his father's passing, at a *yahrtzeit* gathering for his sister, while speaking to his nephews and nieces, Zalman reflected on the experience of taking over the business:

"[I was] thrown in *azoi* [like this] overnight, thrown in to go to work," he said in 2006. "This was something new to me, and I didn't know how and what."

He recalled driving to work in the family station wagon with his mother, picking up some fabric, and selling it. Before he knew it, he had purchased a building. "I remember thinking to myself then, 'What's going on? How come [it is] so successful?' I couldn't believe it myself, you know? . . . I was in a dreamworld."

At the time, he assumed his success was the result of his dedication to the Rebbe. Whatever the Rebbe asked of the Chassidim, Zalman said, "I took it serious. . . . Whatever it was, I used to get involved." These efforts were in addition to the regular donations he gave. "There were times I used to have to go and borrow money to keep this commitment."

Still, he admitted, he had many friends who were similarly devoted to the Rebbe and had not experienced the same level of success.

As he had cared for many orphans over the years, Zalman assured his nephews and nieces that their mother was still watching them from above, helping them along the way. His own success, he was sure, was due to the Rebbe's blessings and his father's intervention on high. "You know, you can really goof up, and he [my father] watches me and he gives me advice and tells me what to do." He had taken risks to grow the business, he said, "because I knew that there was somebody backing me, somebody over there."

Part V

The Family Man

FATHER FIGURE

The period following their father's passing was a difficult one for the Deitsch family. While Zalman kept his grief at bay by throwing himself into his work, his daily Torah study schedule, and family life, his mother and siblings could not ignore the gaping hole in their lives where a caring spouse and father had once been. It became clear to Zalman that he would need to take his father's place at home as well as at work, and with his new wife's blessing, he assumed the role of head of his mother's household.

After her husband's passing, it was very challenging for Mirel Deitsch to work as the administrator of the business. When Zalman realized that his mother was reluctant to come to the office, he began picking her up each morning. His persistence kept her an integral part of the business beyond the age of seventy.

"The responsibility that I had as a mother," Mirel wrote,

Clockwise: Zalman, Yosef, Avrohom Moshe, Shula Schwartz,
Tsevie Gopin, and Rochel Leah Schusterman.

"forced me to continue my life and to raise my children as best as I could."

For many years, almost every evening, rain or shine, Zalman, accompanied by his wife, made his way to her home, where he would check in with his mother and spend time visiting with her.

His devotion to his mother is also evident in his many letters to the Rebbe, where he would include a request for a blessing for her.

Soon Zalman and Cyrel's first child, Toby, was born, followed a year later by Sholom Yeshaya. Despite these new responsibilities, Zalman continued to care for his mother and his siblings. He encouraged his brother Avrohom Moshe, eight years his junior, in his studies, asking him about what he was learning and offering him incentives to learn *Tanya* and Mishnayos by heart. Among the prizes were photos of the Rebbe, which were rare at the time.

When his siblings reached marriageable age, Zalman took

care of all of their needs, from vetting potential shidduchim to purchasing a home for his siblings in Crown Heights. (His sister Alta Shula was already married to Rabbi Shlomo Schwartz, known as "Schwartzie," in 1968. In 1970 they became shluchim at the UCLA campus in Los Angeles, California.)

In the winter of 1970, Zalman's sister Rochel Leah was suggested as a potential match to Gershon Shusterman, a young student in the Lubavitch Yeshivah in 770. Gershon asked the Rebbe in yechidus if he should pursue the suggestion. "She comes from a *Chassidishe* home, and her brothers are fine bochurim and upstanding people," he recalled the Rebbe telling him (see Bava Basra 110a).

Gershon had already received *semichah* and asked the Rebbe if he should study for *dayanus* before getting married. The Rebbe said that he should, "and afterward you should take interest in the shidduch."

Not long after Gershon received dayanus, he and Rochel Leah became engaged. As a married couple they moved to Long Beach, California, where they were among the founders of the Chabad Hebrew Academy, until today a successful Jewish day school, and built a thriving Jewish community with many *baalei teshuvah*.

The youngest child in the Deitsch family, Tsevie, was eleven years old when Zalman married. "Any question that I had, I would turn to him. It was more a child-parent relationship than that of siblings," she said. Zalman encouraged her to make friends who would have a positive influence on her. He also urged her to take on some of her mother's responsibilities, which she did more and more over the years.

When she turned seventeen, he taught her how to drive so that she could better help her mother, he said. She recalled how he would sit in the passenger seat with the Rebbe's sichos while she practiced with her permit. From time to time, he would tell

The engagement celebration of Shula Deitsch and Shlomo Schwartz.

her, "Turn at the next corner; make a right here." Then he would return to his learning.

"I soon realized that he would never ask me to turn left," she said. "He was always looking at the positive in life, the right side." After taking a few right turns, she found herself back in the place where she had started. She told her brother that she wanted more variety in the streets they were taking, and he agreed, but somehow figured out a way not to use the word *left*.

After she graduated from high school, Tsevie was invited to tour Israel with her friends for six weeks, but Zalman had ingrained the responsibility to care for her mother so deeply in her that she hesitated. "I didn't know if I would be able to join them," she said. "Who would assist my mother during that time?" In the end, Zalman took on additional duties so that she could go.

Over the next ten years, Zalman's other siblings found shidduchim and got married. His brother Yosef married Chana Rosenfeld, Tsevie married Gavriel Gopin, and Avrohom Moshe married Rishe Gordon. "Avrohom Moshe got married several months after me," Tsevie said. "Together with my mother, he [Zalman] purchased a home for both of us on Crown Street."

Zalman took care of all the necessary renovations and helped the two couples move into two separate apartments in the home. "He sent us into our future life equipped with all of our needs, with the least amount of stress possible," Tsevie said.

Shortly after his sister-in-law Rishe joined the family, Zalman told her, "Rishe, it is true that you do not have a father-in-law, but I want you to know, if there is anything you need, you can always come to me, and I will do all in my ability to assist."

Over the years, when an issue arose, Rishe knew Zalman was there to help. "Thank you for asking," he would tell her when she approached him. "Let's see what we can do."

She recalled that Zalman once held one of her children on his lap for several hours during a flight. "It was natural to receive a call from him at least once a week to ask how we were doing."

Rishe eventually became the editor of the N'shei Chabad Newsletter. "[Zalman] would call me after every issue came out, and he would praise what he felt was good and comment on what needed to be corrected," she said. She appreciated that he was straightforward with his criticism so that she could work to improve the magazine.

"In any area, when he saw something that he felt needed to be improved, he would gently discuss it with me."

When Cyrel's sister Zlati (Mochkin) needed a place to stay in Crown Heights while she attended school, it was somehow a foregone conclusion that she would live with Zalman and Cyrel. Zlati said she doesn't know many people who would give up all of their privacy for six years so that an out-of-town sister-in-law could stay in their home.

"It was not just that he welcomed me into their house," she said.

"He helped me with anything I needed, including my studies. He was like an older brother to me."

Joining the Business

Over the years, Zalman's siblings married and joined the business while the matriarch, Mrs. Mirel Deitsch, continued to do the bookkeeping. The family members also took an active role in the distribution of profits to tzedakah.

Mirel Deitsch.

When Yosef got married, initially he intended to go on shlichus, but the Rebbe instructed him to join the business, "with a condition that both wives agree to the partnership." After receiving their blessing, in 1976 he became a partner. Several years later, Zalman's brother-in-law Gavriel Gopin also joined the family business at the Rebbe's direction.

When Zalman's younger brother Avrohom Moshe got married in 1978, he asked the Rebbe what he should do, "Spread Judaism or perhaps enter the business world?" The Rebbe directed him to join the business and spread Judaism in his free time.

Under Zalman's guidance, they succeeded in expanding the

The Deitsch Textiles team (from left): Gavriel Gopin, Yosef, Zalman, and Avrohom Moshe.

business. Avrohom Moshe recalled how when he started, he was helping the workers on the floor, cutting fabric and packing orders. One day Zalman called him to the office. "You are not needed on the floor," he said. "For that we hired workers who do the work more quickly than you and cost us less."

It was his job to expand the business, he told his brother. Zalman printed business cards and told him to go to the garment district in Manhattan: "Go from building to building, floor to floor, and meet people. Give them a business card and tell them to contact you if they want to sell or purchase something. Ask if they have any closeouts or if they want to purchase any closeouts."

Avrohom Moshe did as he was asked, but when he returned to the office and asked his mother if he had received any calls from people he had met, she said no. He continued the trips for a few weeks, until he ran out of business cards. He sat with Zalman to plan what to do next. "Zalman thought for a minute," Avrohom Moshe recalled, "and said, 'We will print more business cards, and this time, instead of coming to the office first, to save time go straight to Manhattan to try to set up meetings.'" They both burst out laughing at the idea to "double" their success.

Then, one day in Manhattan, Avrohom Moshe met a high-ranking employee of a garment company who said that he did want to sell something, and invited him into his office. He had two truckloads of fabric that he wanted to sell, he said. Sensing that it was a good deal, Avrohom Moshe said he wanted to purchase the material.

A short while later, they found a customer who liked the material and wanted to purchase the entire stock. Avrohom Moshe continued the relationship with the supplier, and the material he supplied sold very well.

Avrohom Moshe slowly learned the ropes of the business under his brother's guidance. "He believed in hard work," he said of Zalman. "He knew how to bring out the best of the other person's talents."

Soon the business had grown so much that they were forced to move to a larger location, and then to an even larger one, eventually purchasing half of a warehouse. Some time later, after receiving the Rebbe's blessing, they purchased the second half. "*Meshane makom, meshane mazel letovah ulivrochah* (One who changes location changes their fortune, for good and blessing)," the Rebbe wrote.

THE FAMILY GROWS

Zalman and Cyrel were blessed with twelve children: Toby, Shaya, Mendy, Nechemia, Levi, Altie, Chessy, Hindy, Rivky, Sruli, Rochel, and Nosson. Zalman invested much of his energy into his children's education.

Zalman felt uncomfortable taking more than a few days off at a time, saying that the more he worked, the more he would have to give for tzedakah. Thus family vacations were mostly limited to short trips, among other places, to Niagara Falls, Philadelphia, Pennsylvania, and museums. When he came home in the evenings, however, he would leave his business at the office, devoting most of his time to his children and Torah study.

There were times when the younger children would already be sleeping when he came home. Cyrel knew that the childcare she provided was her partnership in the business, as well as the tzedakah that was given from its profits.

Zalman and Cyrel with their children. Top row (left to right): Levi, Nechemia, Mendel, Shaya, (son-in-law) Mendy, and Toby Bernstein. Bottom row: Hindy Mintz, Rivky Vcherashansky, Chessy, Cyrel, Rochel Eisenberg, Zalman, Nosson, Altie Wolvovsky, and Sruli.

When the older children ate supper with their parents, the conversation centered on what the children had done that day. Zalman, in the relaxed atmosphere, would discuss what they were learning. Knowing that their father would request a full report, the children made extra efforts in their schoolwork so that they could answer his questions and have good news to share at the table. As the younger children grew older, the suppers took much longer. Zalman would review the Gemara with the *mefarshim* beforehand, and a lively discussion would commence. The children knew that the best time to get help with a difficult passage or topic in their studies was in the evening hours.

When the children asked for help with personal issues they had with their classmates, Zalman encouraged them to approach their fellow students with love, and avoid quarrels. He always greeted his children's friends and made sure they felt comfortable.

Zalman with his daughters Hindy and Rivki.

When he noticed that a classmate of his children needed something, he would discreetly try to arrange it, like the time he purchased a new pair of glasses for one of his son's classmates.

Cleanliness, orderliness, and good manners were very important to him. He often reminded his children to tuck in their shirts and pick up after themselves.

His daughters recalled that when they went shopping, he would compliment them on the quality and modesty of their clothes, always wanting them to look their best.

As the children grew older, they came to understand that just as their father demanded the utmost of himself, he expected it of them as well. It was a special day in the Deitsch home when report cards arrived. Zalman would review each one in detail, give compliments, and express surprise when a mark was lower than he expected. Seeing how much their father cared, the children came away determined not to disappoint him in the future.

When his sons went to out-of-town yeshivahs, he continued

to follow their progress, studying the Gemara they were learning that year so that it would be fresh in his mind. Their conversations on the phone always centered on their studies. From time to time, he would ask them to write down what they were learning and fax it to the office. His office staff attested that when these faxes arrived, he would stop his work and review them immediately, taking great pleasure in what they wrote.

Zalman encouraged his daughters to study music.

As he had done with his siblings, he offered his children incentives to learn passages of *Tanya* or Mishnayos by heart. Every milestone in their studies was a cause for celebration.

He encouraged his daughters to learn to play the piano and develop their talents. While he never wanted anyone to sit idle, the only time family members could recall him relaxing on the couch with a cup of coffee was when he listened to his daughter play a nigun on the piano.

His children learned from his example the importance of creating a schedule for every day that included a set study regimen.

A motto that personified his own approach to life, Zalman

would often repeat the mantra of his grandmother Hinda Deitsch, "*Men foyelt zich trachten,*" don't be too lazy to think.

Every night, once the children were in bed, he would go into his private study on the first floor, where he would sit and learn. The children fell asleep to the sound of his studies. They knew that this was his private time, and he should not be disturbed. Even so, if he heard that they were having a hard time falling asleep, he would go upstairs and tell them Chassidishe stories, of which he knew many.

As the children grew older and stayed awake later, Zalman would spend time in meaningful conversation with them.

Once, when he was asked how he could fit so much into a day, he said, "I go to sleep on time." Even when his house was full of people, he would quietly slip away and go to bed. "To go to bed on time takes more *mesiras nefesh* than waking up on time," he would say, quoting the famed Chassid Reb Mendel Futerfas, who worked with self-sacrifice to maintain Chabad underground schools in the Soviet Union.

The Special Day

On Shabbos, Zalman dedicated himself to his family. He spent more time with his children, giving them Chassidishe life lessons and making it an enjoyable day for everyone.

"He would come home visibly tired from work," said David Eagle, a regular guest in the Deitsch home in the late 1970s. "But that did not matter. Everything from work, the weekday, dropped" the moment he entered the house, sometimes only half an hour before Shabbos. "It was tough for him to stay up , yet he learned and sang with the kids. You could see that it was the highlight of his week."

On winter Friday nights, when shul ended early, a group would gather at the Deitsch home to study one of the Rebbe's talks. Seated around the table, each person took a turn to read a few paragraphs and summarize what the Rebbe was saying, Mr. Eagle recalled. Unable to read the Hebrew, however, he did not participate. Eventually, he took a break from college to attend Yeshivah Tiferes Bachurim in Morristown, New Jersey, where he gained the necessary skills. From then on, whenever he visited the Deitsches, he took his turn to read from the *sichah*. "Zalman took such nachas," he said.

With his son Mendy.

Early in the morning, after going to the mikvah, Zalman would attend a shiur by Reb Yoel Kahan on *Samech Vov*, a voluminous series of Chassidic discourses by the Rebbe Rashab, the fifth Chabad Rebbe, which details many fundamental and deep Chassidic concepts. The class would later alternate between the homes of the participants.

After the Rebbe's wife, Rebbetzin Chaya Mushka, passed away in 5748 (1988), the Rebbe encouraged people to do good deeds in her memory. Zalman decided that he would institute a new custom in his home: to review by heart a maamar of the Rebbe at the

Shabbos table every week. He asked each of his older sons to learn one chapter of a specific maamar by heart every week and then review it at the table. At first, it was the latest *"mugah"* maamar, which had been edited by the Rebbe and published. If there was no recent one, and after the Rebbe's stroke, they would choose one together.

During the week, Zalman would choose the maamar, arrange for copies to be made for each child, and try to learn it together with the children. "The maamar brought this cohesive feeling of studying into the home," said his daughter Toby. "It was not just last minute. We saw that it was something that was important to him."

After they completed their chapters, he set an example by pledging to memorize the rest himself. When his children married, their spouses participated in the project as well. To Zalman's delight, the younger children also expressed interest in participating. Some learned just one line; others learned more. His youngest son, Nosson, began participating at the age of ten.

Over the years, many who participated in the Shabbos table at the Deitsch home commented on the impact the recitation of the maamar had on them.

Cyrel, who had been a boarding student herself when she studied at Beth Rivkah in Crown Heights, knew what it felt like to be away from home, especially over Shabbos, and encouraged her children in high school to bring out-of-town guests to their home for Shabbos. Over the years, the out-of-towners learned that the Deitsch home was open to them, and the table was always full.

They also had many guests from the two schools in Crown Heights for recent returnees to Jewish observance, Hadar Hatorah and Machon Chana. For their benefit, Zalman always made a point of explaining in a simple, clear manner whatever was being discussed in the maamar.

Singing and dancing with his children on Chanukah.

He would ask everyone to prepare and say a *dvar Torah* at the table. His niece Chanel Lipskier, who was a classmate of one of Zalman's daughters, recalled how he would tell them each to say one part of the dvar Torah they had prepared in school.

Love for Song

Sometimes he would ask guests to sing a nigun as well. Once, a guest from Kfar Chabad sang the soul-stirring, "*Nigun Hagaguim*," by Reb Zalman Zlatopolsky. Zalman was captivated by the guest's performance. After Shabbos, he asked the young man to record it so he could listen to it again, as if he did not already know it.

The walk to shul on Shabbos was an opportunity to teach his children new melodies, and he encouraged them to sing out loud with him. "He was never bashful to sing out loud while walking in a mostly non-Jewish section of Crown Heights," his son Mendy said.

After the Rebbe had a stroke in 1992, thousands of Chassidim gathered at the Ohel of the Previous Rebbe, asking the Rebbe

Rayatz to daven for the Rebbe's health and speedy recovery.

Speeches were made, petitions read out loud, and nigunim sung. Usually, they sang the most famous nigun of each rebbe. But on one occasion, when Zalman's son Nechemia was present, there was a change. Instead of "*Yemin Hashem*," for the Tzemach Tzedek, Rabbi Yoel Kahan began to sing the "*Nigun Hishtatchus*."

It was an appro-

Studying with his daughter Rivky.

priate choice: When the Alter Rebbe was very sick, and his life was in danger, his daughter, Rebbetzin Devorah Leah, had asked G-d to take her life instead.[1] She then passed away. Her son, the Tzemach Tzedek, later the third Chabad rebbe, was from then on raised by his grandparents, the Alter Rebbe and Rebbetzin Sterna. When visiting his mother's resting place, he would sing this powerful melody.

The melody was not well-known, however. Most of the crowd was silent while Reb Yoel sang. When Nechemia got home that day, he asked his father if he knew it. Replying that he did, Zalman

---

1. See the story at length in *Sefer Hatoldos Admur Hazaken*, vol. 2, pp. 463; *Likutei Diburim*, vol. 4, p. 1330.

offered to record a tape of it. Nechemia listened to it many times until he had mastered it.

Educational Priorities

Zalman seldom used any form of punishment for misbehavior because he found that encouragement, praise, and incentives were more effective tools. If the children were acting up, he would go over to them and quietly ask them to behave—they were quick to listen.

Zlati Mochkin once observed some of the Deitsch children doing something mischievous. Zalman called them over and asked, "Do you think that this is the way to act?" She commented that the children melted "from the authoritative tone and fatherly love with which the message was delivered."

Rishe once explained that she had learned a valuable lesson about how to deal with sibling rivalry from her brother-in-law. "Zalman went to the room where he heard the arguing and closed the door on them. He let them learn how to deal with their issues on their own."

She also recalled how she once went with Zalman and his family to Camp Emunah to visit her sister. There were six Deitsch kids in the minivan. At the time there were no seatbelt laws, so there was a lot of action in the back. "Zalman and Cyrel, despite the ruckus behind them, continued having a quiet discussion," Rishe said. When one of the children popped their head into the front seat to ask something, Zalman placed his finger on his lips and answered, "Mommy is talking."

Cyrel brought calm to the family, Rishe said. Once, while returning from a trip,, the children grew thirsty and started nagging their mother for water. At the moment she had no way to give any to them. "Cyrel turned around, and I was expecting her to raise her voice and admonish them for their constant nagging," she said. But Cyrel just told them calmly, "I understand, I am also very thirsty." Her empathy was enough to quiet them down.

When Zalman wanted the boys to do some chores in the house, he would call them over to have a meeting with them. "It always worked," Cyrel said. "They did what he asked without any complaining."

Some of the children had their challenges with school. Rather than just rely on hired tutors or professionals, Zalman involved himself heavily in the academic issues as they arose. When one of his sons had difficulty reading, he spent hours practicing with him. He understood that it would be impossible for the child to daven the full davening, and so encouraged him to increase the amount slowly over time. His effort, attention, and patience gave the child the confidence to overcome his challenge.

Zalman constantly encouraged his children to strive for more. Once, a class was being split up according to the children's academic levels. The school put one of the Deitsches' sons into the higher class. Not happy about it, the boy complained to his parents about the extra work that would be required.

"If they placed you in a higher class, it is a sign that you need to raise your level of study," his father told him. "You have to study diligently until you reach what is expected of you. Do not choose the easy way out."

When one of his children began to use improper language, Zalman took him aside and explained that it is not befitting for a Chassidishe child to speak that way. "To help yourself overcome this habit, place a limit on yourself in how you speak. Get used to it slowly," he suggested.

He advised his son that every time he caught himself using inappropriate language, he should put a quarter from his personal allowance into the *pushka*. The boy agreed. After a while, when he realized that his money was disappearing, he made a greater effort

On a trip to Niagara Falls, 1998.

to improve his language until the problem was corrected.

Toby said that her father would seldom chastise them for bad behavior. "It was quiet expectations. He trusted that we would do the right thing." When she once did do something wrong, he made sure she rectified the situation. "I am disappointed," he told her. She never did it again.

Another time, one of the children began taking money from his parents without permission. The boy was also shoplifting items that he wanted from stores. After explaining that the Torah forbids such behaviors, Zalman pointed out to his son, "You do not want others taking your money or things, do you? Others also do not like it." The strategy worked and he stopped.

Then Zalman suggested they create a list of all the things he had taken, and from whom, and return them. The boy protested that he no longer had the items, so Zalman said he would give him a loan. "You will repay it with the money you will receive from studying Torah by heart," he said.

The child was still too embarrassed to return the items. "It is said that the items need to be returned," he told his father, "but nowhere does it say that the one to whom the items belong has to know who took them."

Zalman studied the relevant halachos with his son, who, it turned out, was right (Bava Kama 64b and Rambam, *Hilchos Geneivah*, ch. 1). The items were then returned without the owner knowing from whom.

There was hardly ever any discussion in the home about all the family tragedies. Whenever Zalman spoke of his father, it was to remark how joyous he was, how he was the life of the party. "He wanted there to be always simchah in the house," Toby said.

She added that the one time he did speak about his pain happened when she was crying about a mark on an exam. "Baruch Hashem you don't have real things to cry about," Zalman told her in a very soft voice. "My tears are all dried up already."

At that moment, she said, he put her life in proper perspective.

A Story with a Cow

Zalman liked to tell his children the parable of the Jewish woman in the shtetl who had to walk far away to fill her buckets with water from a well. She would schlep the buckets back home and use the water sparingly until she needed to go get more.

After Shabbos, she would use water to clean the cholent pot, and then to clean the floor of her house. When she was done, she would give the water to the cow. The cow would especially enjoy the taste of the *Motzei Shabbos* water, flavored by cholent and leftovers from the delicious Shabbos meal, and looked forward to this weekly treat. However, once when she accidently kicked over the bucket, the cow was disappointed when it received regular water.

The woman went to bed, but the cow could not fall asleep, wondering what had happened to its delicious water. Finally, the

The bar mitzvah of Levi at the Kosel.

cow concluded, "I know what happened. She must have enjoyed the water herself."

"Let's not be like the cow," Zalman would say. "We should not assume that whatever we like, the other person likes, or that whatever we don't like the other person does not like either. Perhaps, what is a treat for you, for the other person may be disgusting."

Educating to Give

The Deitsches lived the average lifestyle, and they never felt that their financial situation was better than that of their friends' families. "He [Zalman] would never let us spend too much on clothes or haircuts," Toby said. Each child had an allowance, which could not be exceeded, for their shopping.

At times she would complain about how her friends' parents let them spend as much as they wanted, but Zalman would merely crack one of his famous half smiles, making it clear that this was an irrelevant argument that made him uncomfortable. "It was useless to complain."

Reading a book to his grandchildren.

Looking for Change

After three years of consecutive bar mitzvahs for three of their children, Cyrel wanted to do something different for their next son, Levi. They would make a small gathering at home and use the money they would have spent on a larger celebration to travel to Eretz Yisroel.

Zalman agreed with the condition that they have the Rebbe's blessing. The question was relayed to the Rebbe through Rabbi Binyomin Klein, one of the Rebbe's secretaries: "Zalman Deitsch would like to make a bar mitzvah in Eretz Yisroel, and while there he will visit the local Chabad institutions."

"*A gleiche zach*" (It is a sensible business idea), the Rebbe responded.

As they were nearing their bar mitzvahs, Zalman encouraged his children to give half the money they received to the Rebbe. The day after he received an aliyah in the Rebbe's minyan (it was during the *shloshim* for the Rebbe's brother-in-law, the Rashag, held in his apartment on the third floor of 770), Levi prepared his donation. It was significantly smaller than his brothers' had been because his event had been smaller—the main celebration would be in Israel. Levi reported this problem to his father.

Zalman told him to wait a day before bringing it to the Rebbe. The next day, he gave his son an additional $1,500 to give to the Rebbe. "Just because we made for you a small event does not mean that the Rebbe should receive less."

Love for Seforim

Zalman's bookcases were bursting with his collection of *seforim* and booklets, which he often had bound into volumes. He dedicated a separate section for his books on Moshiach, labeling them the "Moshiach Library."

There was a bookseller who came to Zalman once in a while to offer some of the latest seforim. Even if Zalman already had some of them, he would buy the newer editions anyway, in order to help the man earn a livelihood. To those who teased him for being a bibliophile, he jokingly responded, "I have 'book knowledge.' I know which seforim I have."

Every Chanukah he would give the children money to purchase seforim, rather than buying them himself, because he wanted them to invest the effort in choosing for themselves.

Once, he told his children that if they could find a sefer that he had two copies of, they could have the extra one. All of the children came away with seforim, except for one, who complained that he had nothing. Zalman told him to choose whichever set he wanted, even if there was no duplicate.

While Zalman himself had simple bookcases, when his children married, to instill a love for seforim, he purchased nice bookcases for them from his brother-in-law Shlomo Ezagui.

Children's Activism

Zalman encouraged his children to participate actively in all the Rebbe's mitzvah campaigns. "He always spoke about how much we need to do what the Rebbe wants," Toby said, adding that her father had a deep-seated desire for them to be active in spreading Yiddishkeit. "We just had this feeling of expectations from us."

On Purim, Zalman often took his children to old age

Zalman with his son Levi before he went on his route to read the *Megillah* on Purim.

homes through a program organized by Tiferet Zekeinim Levi Yitzchak. There he arranged for someone to read the *Megillah*, and the children sang or made plays for the residents. When his children were older, he encouraged them to learn how to read the *Megillah* on their own.

Zalman was thrilled when his son Nechemia told him about the campaign among the yeshiva students: they planned to deliver copies of the Rebbe's latest published talks to shuls in Borough Park, where the residents would not otherwise have access to them. He immediately offered his car for their use, and on Thursday nights when the talks were printed, Nechemia and his friends

Zalman at Megilah reading for those who could not make it to a shul on Purim.

would make their rounds.

If the shul was closed, the students left the booklets in a bag on the door handle. To protect them from rain and snow, special bags were manufactured with one side taller than the other.

The campaign was mentioned in a weekly report to the Rebbe, who responded, "It was received. With thanks. You should continue to report good news, with addition [in the activities]. The time is opportune [for the campaign]. I will mention you at the resting place of the Rebbe Rayatz."

On one of their runs, the young men got into a small accident. With some trepidation, Nechemia called his father to tell him what had happened. Zalman wasn't upset, however. "Thank G-d no one was hurt. We will pay whatever we need to, and everything will be okay," he told his son. Over time, more cars were added to the delivery routes, one sent to Flatbush and another to Queens. Today the program has expanded to include all the Jewish neighborhoods in New York City.

EXTENDING
THE FAMILY

Zalman's special care for his siblings included their children as well. Living in California, his nephews from the Schwartz and Shusterman families knew they had a home in Crown Heights, and some lived for many years with their uncle and aunt when they came to New York for school. Zalman treated them like his own children, taking an interest in their studies and talking with them at the supper table.

"I always felt I was part of the family," said Rabbi Mayshe Schwartz, today a shliach in Brookline, Massachusetts. "I never felt like an outsider, a second-class citizen, a nephew versus son. I was completely, completely welcomed."

Zalman's nephew Shaya (Rishe and Avrohom Moshe's son) lived in Crown Heights. "One day, Zalman showed up unexpectedly at our home," Rishe related, "and sat Shaya on the couch. We didn't know what it was about, and we all stood around waiting to see why he came."

Zalman said he had been in Oholei Torah that day and saw a chart of Mishnayos *baal peh* where Shaya had been listed. "I see that you learned a lot by heart, and you should know that we are proud of you," he said. Zalman pulled out a one hundred-dollar bill and gave it to him.

With his nephew Nissan Deitsch.

When Shaya was a teenager, Zalman established a set time to learn *Samach Vov* with the young man. Shaya found it difficult to come on time and, like a typical teenager, occasionally did not show up. Zalman never gave up on him, however. Whenever he did not come, he would call his home and ask what happened.

Being part of the family came with privileges, Rabbi Schwartz said—"I was able to raid the fridge and the cake corner like anybody else"—and with responsibilities. A few days after he arrived, he went to the kitchen and saw a list on the fridge with the names of all the Deitsch children and which chapter of the maamar everyone should review and know by heart to recite at the Shabbos table.

"I noticed that my name was on the same list." He recalled feeling a combination of anxiety and pride, "honored that Zalman thought of me in that high light." He spent a lot of time preparing his chapter. "I got a lot of compliments and a kiss."

Another one of Zalman's nephews was having a difficult time

in school. When it came time for him to transfer to a *beis midrash*, Zalman advised that he be sent to a specific out-of-town yeshiva. "The learning there is on a higher level," he told them. "They are very schedule-oriented and disciplined. This is the perfect place for him."

The yeshiva, however, did not want to accept him. Zalman used his influence, and eventually they did accept him. True to his predictions, the boy was very successful there. Today, his nephew, a shliach of the Rebbe, is appreciative that Zalman went out of his way to help him fulfill his potential.

As his nieces and nephews began to marry, Zalman continued to play the role of a father, and even a father-in-law. His niece Chanel married Motty Lipskier, who had lost his father at a young age. Zalman took it upon himself to be extra friendly to him, encouraging him to use his talents to the fullest.

When one of his sons married a young woman who had lost a parent, Zalman sat with her, explaining how she should prepare spiritually for the wedding. "He took it so naturally to help me and prepare me accordingly," she said.

"I was very influenced by my time there," Rabbi Schwartz said of his years in the Deitsch home. He named one of his sons after the uncle who "materially and spiritually thought of me as one of his own, and I felt it."

LIFE IN
REFOCUS

T hough Zalman experienced much tragedy in his life, it was the Rebbe's teachings that helped him avoid sinking into bitterness and depression by looking ahead and working toward a brighter future.

On 17 Av 5737 (1977), Zalman's sister Alta Shula Schwartz collapsed unconscious during a wedding in Los Angeles. The *kallah*, who was a doctor, performed CPR, but efforts to revive her were unsuccessful. The twenty-nine-year-old mother left behind seven orphans and much pain.

Nine years later, on 4 Nissan 5746 (1986), Zalman's sister Rochel Leah Shusterman went to perform at a school Pesach production. On the way back, she did not feel well, and an hour later passed away at the age of thirty-six. She left eleven young children, including a set of one-year-old twins.

The matriarch of the family, Mirel, wrote to the Rebbe with

Zalman and Cyrel (right) with Shlomo and Alta Shula Schwartz

a broken heart: "Why did G-d do this?" A response was quick to arrive, expressing perplexity, the Rebbe wrote, "??!" on the general letter:

> It is understood that there is no time at all for all of this [questioning]—for there needs to be an effort by every one of them [the family] to make the children's and widowers', *sheyichyu*, lives more pleasant, and not to investigate the ways of Hashem. I will mention this at the resting place [of the Previous Rebbe].

Eight years later, on 27 Tammuz 5754 (1994), during the shloshim for the Rebbe, Mirel returned from her great-grandson's bris and said she didn't feel well. She went to the office of the family doctor, Eli Rosen, where she collapsed and was rushed to the hospital. She never regained consciousness and passed away at the age of seventy-three.

Zalman made an obvious effort to overcome his own pain as much as possible so that he could care for the rest of the family. When one of his daughters asked him why he had not cried much, he responded, "The tears have dried up." Mirel was laid to rest in the first row of the women's section across from the Ohel. Her *matzeiva* tells of her self-sacrifice for the education of her children and how, "*Meod tziptza legilui haMoshiach*" (She fervently awaited the revelation of Moshiach).

The resting place of Mirel Deitsch.

Part VI

Merging Two Worlds

DEDICATED CHASSID

At his farbrengens, the Rebbe would share words of Torah on the parsha, *nigleh*, and Chassidus, talk about current events (especially about the situation in the Land of Israel), give directives, and inspire the crowd to do more good in the world. It was a time for Chassidim to bask in the Rebbe's presence and absorb his teachings. Zalman never missed an opportunity to attend.

Since many farbrengens were on Shabbos, the Rebbe's talks were memorized, then transcribed, printed, and distributed afterward for study. The Rebbe would also edit many of these farbrengens.

Generally, farbrengens were announced before Shabbos, but the Rebbe occasionally made his intention to speak known on Shabbos morning. Zalman arranged to have someone come to the shul where he davened and inform him about these impromptu

Receiving lekach and a booklet from the Rebbe, 1989.

farbrengens.

On the days when the Rebbe spoke, Zalman cut short his lengthy davening so that he could go home and make Kiddush for the family before heading to his customary place in 770 for the farbrengen. During the singing between each of the talks, when many Chassidim would lift cups of wine to the Rebbe to say l'chaim, Zalman very rarely joined in. He felt that it was not right to take up the Rebbe's precious time, he told his family, even the moment it took to respond to such a gesture.

After the conclusion of the farbrengen, no matter how late the hour, Zalman would stay and listen to the *chazarah*, review of the farbrengen by the *chozrim*, a select few individuals who would memorize and repeat the Rebbe's talks so that they could be accurately recorded. When his children were old enough, he encouraged them by example to stay for the chazarah as well.

During the summer, when many in the Crown Heights community travelled upstate to the Catskills, Zalman remained in town on Shabbos Mevorchim, when the Rebbe would regularly farbreng. In addition, if he had a reason to believe that there would be a farbrengen on another Shabbos, he would stay. It was for this reason that, at a certain point, it was decided that it would be best for them all to remain in the city the entire summer, which they did from 1977 onward.

According to his family, one of the few farbrengens Zalman partially missed was on the Shabbos of 19 Sivan 1988, when he left in the middle to accompany Cyrel to the hospital, where she gave birth to their youngest son, Nosson.

In addition to the farbrengens, Zalman would have preferred to daven on Shabbos with the Rebbe's minyan in 770, yet he heeded the Rebbe's call to support the smaller shuls in Crown Heights, many of which, after the white flight in the 1960s and '70s, were struggling to survive. On Friday night, he attended the Skverer

Zalman (center) waiting for the Rebbe to come in for a farbrengen.

shtiebel on Kingston Avenue, today Bais Eliezer Yitzchak and Mikvah Meir, and on Shabbos day, the Reines Shul on Troy Avenue,
where Mesivta Oholei Torah is located.

On Shabbos Mevorchim, however, when the Chabad custom
is to recite the entire Tehillim in shul before davening, Zalman
would take the opportunity to go to 770 and recite Tehillim with
the Rebbe's minyan. He made sure to go to the mikvah beforehand
and be there on time. "Be there at 8:30," he would tell his children,
before the Rebbe enters, "so you should be ready for the Rebbe,
and the Rebbe should not wait for you."

Reviewing the Talks

For the first several years of his marriage, until 1976, shortly after
making Havdalah, Zalman would sit down to write notes on what
the Rebbe had said that day. He filled many notebooks over the
years. In 1977, a group of students undertook to publish the Rebbe's talks after Shabbos in an organized and timely manner. Zalman no longer found it necessary to document his own detailed

notes, though he encouraged his children to take their own notes as a way of internalizing what they had heard.

He himself would listen to tapes of the Rebbe's weekday talks and the Shabbos farbrengen (these were repeated after Shabbos by Rabbi Yoel Kahan, the chief chozer) whenever he had a free moment. Even before cars had tape players, he purchased a battery-operated tape recorder for his car.

On yom tov, following the tahalucha, when many would go from Crown Heights to other communities to share words of Chassidus in the shuls there, the Rebbe would often greet Chassidim outside 770 as they returned. On Shavuos in 5751 (1991), the Rebbe, standing outside 770, gave a brief talk as they came back. Many had trouble hearing what the Rebbe said. Zalman's son Mendel happened to be close to the Rebbe, and afterward assisted those who were reviewing the talk, much to Zalman's pride and delight.

When another son, Nechemia, was sixteen, he once expressed a desire to purchase a complete set of tapes of the Rebbe's sichos. Zalman, overjoyed, offered to loan him the money. "He wanted it not to be a gift," Nechemia said. "He wanted me to treasure the tapes that would come through my own effort." He repaid his father over the next few years with the money he earned working as a camp counselor.

When his children married, Zalman advised them to listen to tapes of farbrengens when they were alone in the car. But if your spouse is with you, he told them, spend the time talking. "Don't be a tzaddik at her expense."

Another piece of marital advice that Zalman gave came from the story of Avraham and Sarah: When the malach informed Sarah and Avraham that they would have a child, Sarah laughed, and Hashem turned to Avraham and asked why she had laughed. "Why not ask Sarah directly?" Zalman asked. "When the wife is

Reb Yoel Kahan reviewing one of the Rebbe's talks.

lacking in emunah, the husband is held responsible."

Learning to Connect

In addition to his regular study sessions and helping his children with their homework, beginning when he arrived home at seven each evening, Zalman dedicated much of his time to Torah study.

Once, Levi saw his father learning a sichah without a connection to the weekly parsha or the time of year. To his inquiry Zalman responded, "You would be correct if the only reason one learns a sichah is to share it at the Shabbos table. However, when one studies a sichah in order to learn what the Rebbe has to teach us, then it does not matter on what topic or time of year it is."

Years later, when Levi opened a Chabad House in Vienna, Virginia, his father asked him if he studied the Rebbe's sichos regularly. He responded that he did, because he had to deliver classes for the community. "I'm referring to learning to have a personal connection with the Rebbe," Zalman said. "To learn just for the sake of learning."

The Rebbe's Messages

Zalman's study of the Rebbe's maamarim and published correspondence intensified after the Rebbe suffered a stroke in 5752 (1992). A few months before Zalman passed away in 5766 (2006), he completed all of the Rebbe's voluminous published teachings in *Likutei Sichos, Sichos Kodesh, Toras Menachem, Igros Kodesh,* and *Reshimos.*

His rigorous study regimen ensured that he always had something to share with the Jewish customers and businesspeople he encountered. Once, a Chassid of the Munkatcher Rebbe walked into his office. "I just read a letter from the Lubavitcher Rebbe to a Munkatch Chassid," Zalman said (*Igros Kodesh,* vol. 21, p. 135). The letter was written to a couple who had requested a blessing for children. "The Rebbe wrote, among other directives, that he [the husband] should, from time to time, envision the Munkatcher Rebbe's face, and that they should make the effort to assist people with their spiritual needs, and Hashem should give them an abundance of material and spiritual sustenance."

To both men's astonishment, it turned out that the Chassid standing in Zalman's office was the son who was born to the couple after receiving that letter. Zalman immediately gave him the volume where the Rebbe's letter to his parents was found.

His schedule also included in-depth study of the Rebbe's maamarim. Whenever an occasion presented itself, he had one ready to repeat from memory. Throughout the year, he had set times when he would deliver a maamar from memory in shul. In addition to his birthday and his parents' yahrtzeits, after 5754 (1994), he would also review one on the Shabbos before Gimmel Tammuz. Once, at a family gathering, he reviewed a maamar by heart, amazing the attendees, including several scholarly Chassidim, who wondered out loud how a businessman could have the time for such deep study.

Learning with his son Mendy.

He would study whenever he had a chance, always keeping a *likut*, the new weekly sichah booklet of the Rebbe's talks, with him. Once, when stopped by a police officer, Zalman told the officer he was rushing to teach a class. The officer asked to see the material he was going to teach. Zalman pulled out the likut, which he had folded in his jacket pocket, and he let him go.

Beginning in 1983, Rabbi Simon Jacobson said, Zalman joined Los Angeles philanthropist Berel Weiss in supporting Vaad Hanochos Hatemimim, which published the Rebbe's Shabbos talks.

At one point, the Rebbe encouraged the study of *Ohr HaTorah*, the discourses of the Tzemach Tzedek, the third Chabad Rebbe (see *Toras Menachem 5750*, vol. 1, p. 336 and *Toras Menachem 5751*, vol. 1, p. 329). The forty-volume set can be intimidating, but Zalman dedicated much energy to understanding the material and writing synopses on almost the entire set.

On special occasions, the Rebbe would distribute booklets or volumes that he wanted people to study. On the 20th of Cheshvan

Learning with Michoel Slavin the night before the bris of
their grandson Yosef Chaim Deitsch.

5750 (1989), the Rebbe distributed *Kuntres Etz Chayim*, by the
Rebbe Rashab, in honor of the hundredth anniversary of the Rebbe Rashab's birthday. Nechemia, then a fifteen-year-old yeshiva
student, had a hard time understanding the content. When he told
his father, Zalman studied one chapter a night with him until they
finished it. "He showed me how to cherish a volume the Rebbe
distributed," Nechemia said.

Rambam Study

In 1984, the Rebbe initiated a campaign to unify Jewish people around the world through the study of the Rambam's seminal
work, the fourteen-volume *Mishneh Torah*, which includes just
under one thousand chapters on Jewish observance. Participants
could choose one of three tracks, depending on their ability—three
chapters a day, one chapter a day, or the brief entry in the *Sefer
Hamitzvos* corresponding to that day's portion of three chapters.

Not surprisingly, Zalman took the Rambam initiative very

Learning and watching his children play in Springfield.

seriously, joining a group of anash that studied three chapters in-depth each evening. In addition, for many years, he personally delivered a daily class on one chapter at his home.

He refused to gloss over complex chapters, such as the laws of sanctifying the new moon (*Kiddush Hachodesh*), which include a discussion of the mathematical calculation of astronomy. Instead, he invited Rabbi Yosef Losh, an expert in the laws, to deliver the class at his home, and afterward spent more time discussing the details with him. Rabbi Yoseph Keller, who would attend the class, would later write a book on the laws of Kiddush Hachodesh.

After completing a section, participants were tested on their knowledge. Zalman's children recall to this day how they were once making noise while their father was preparing for the difficult test, and he rebuked them. It was so unusual for him to speak that way that they realized what he was doing had to be extremely important.

Zalman participated in and often contributed toward the large

In his home study.

celebration marking the completion of the entire *Mishneh Torah*. He was also a regular sponsor of the smaller events in honor of completing the individual volumes.

Torah Study

In addition to the class on Rambam, Zalman had a weekly study session with Avi Baitelman, a friend and local electrician. On Friday nights, after a long week, they studied in a "block shiur" the sichah that had been published that week. Zalman insisted that the Friday night class continue also during the summer, which meant it ended close to midnight. Cyrel would prepare special pastries and tea for the class.

According to Chabad teachings, Zalman told his children, one must be completely engrossed in whatever task was at hand. Thus, he would make an effort not to interrupt his studies to answer the phone or the doorbell. In good weather, his favorite place to study was the back porch. "Why would I need to go upstate during the summer when we have the porch?" he often said. That cherished space was also the scene of many conversations with his children about their studies and their personal lives.

Zalman's sons-in-law recall that, in addition to their more mundane conversations, he took particular pleasure in discussing their Torah study with them. If he felt they were not devoting enough time to learning, he would ask them to help him find a specific topic within the Rebbe's teachings as a way of nudging them in the right direction.

Study well, Zalman would say. If the Rebbe will stop you one day in the street and ask you about a specific detail in something you studied, you should be able to answer. In fact, he related, this had actually happened to Rabbi Herschel Fogelman. The longtime shliach to Worcester, Massachusetts, was known for studying the weekly portion of the Alter Rebbe's *Torah Ohr* and *Likutei Torah*. Every Shabbos he would teach it to his congregation.

The Rebbe once stopped him in the street and asked if he knew the opening words of that week's *Torah Ohr*. It was the parsha of *Terumah,* and though the *Torah Ohr* usually began with a verse from the parsha, that week the verse was from *Shir Hashirim.* Rabbi Fogelman immediately answered with the correct verse, and the Rebbe smiled with appreciation.

ALL WELCOME

As Crown Heights residents, the Deitsches opened their home and supported the Rebbe's shluchim in whatever ways they could. The International Conference of Shluchim was a special time for Zalman. "Those days are among the most delightful days for me on the calendar," he wrote one year. "Just the meeting of family, friends, neighbors, and acquaintances, who during the year are in some corner of the globe, is a good reason to uplift one's mood. If you add to that the wondrous and miraculous stories they have to tell, it is as if the entire time they are here, we are given an additional soul."

Zalman knew that his mission was to be in the business world, but he also took an active part in all the Rebbe's campaigns to promote Jewish observance. In a 1985 letter to the Rebbe, he asked that his activities should give the Rebbe nachas, "and I should have

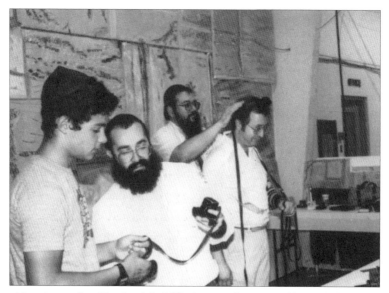

Mivtzoim at an Israel Day Parade in California, 1983. Also seen is Rabbi Yitzchok Marcus.

the strength and fortitude to fulfill them."

Tefillin Campaign

On Zalman's desk at the warehouse there was always a pair of tefillin ready to be put on anyone who had not yet done the mitzvah that day. The businessman had his ways of convincing the reluctant to roll up their sleeves and put on tefillin. If he felt that a person was committed enough, he would encourage him to purchase his own pair, at times subsidizing the cost. He also helped yeshiva students who would go out weekly on mivtzoim with purchasing pairs to use on their routes.

One day, he received a call from someone whom he had helped put on tefillin a few days before. The man was very emotional and told him that the same day he put on tefillin, he had been in a grave car accident. A truck had rammed into his car from behind and completely crushed it.

The rescue teams could not believe that anyone could have survived, "but I exited the car unscathed. They took me for check-ups and I was fine." The man said that he had recalled at that moment what Zalman had quoted him from Gemara (Menachos 36b), "The one who puts on tefillin, his days are lengthened."

"I'm calling to thank you for saving my life," the man concluded.

Mezuzah Campaign

At the farbrengen marking the Previous Rebbe's yahrtzeit and the Rebbe's ascent to leadership on the 10th of Shevat, 5734 (1974), the Rebbe initiated the *mezuzah* campaign, a call to assure that all Jewish homes should affix mezuzos (associated with divine protection) on their doorposts and to check the validity of all mezuzos already installed.

Over three months later, Palestinian terrorists attacked an elementary school in the town of Ma'alot, Israel, taking 105 students and ten teachers as hostages. In the course of the rescue, tragically, twenty-five children and teachers were murdered. After the event, the Rebbe called to intensify the campaign.

When his brother Avrohom Moshe completed a year in kollel after his marriage, the Rebbe instructed him to join the family business and spread Judaism during his free time. Avrohom Moshe approached the Lubavitch Youth Organization in New York and asked if he could assist in the mezuzah campaign. They provided him with the names of people in the area who needed mezuzos. As the lists grew, Avrohom Moshe recruited others in Crown Heights to join him in the work.

Shmuel Brook helped organize and recruit more volunteers, and hired Rabbi Moshe Nissan Wolvovsky to direct the efforts. Eventually, Gavriel Gopin joined the committee, and together they took Mivtzah Mezuzah to a new level.

At this point, Zalman, never one to stand by the wayside when it came to the Rebbe's campaigns, offered his basement rent-free as

Receiving lekach from the Rebbe.

an official office. At the office, volunteers received briefcases with mezuzos and all the tools needed to remove old mezuzos and hang up new ones.

Zalman helped the committee pay the salaries for Rabbi Wolvovsky and later Yosef Meizlish, who replaced him. Eventually, after Rabbi Meizlish left, Rabbi Shmuel Kesselman was put in charge of day-to-day operations, and though the organization is now financially independent, they continue to use the Deitsch basement, free of charge, until today.

A separate door was built, and the office was busy from early in the morning until late (the Deitsches never complained about the noise). Representatives visit over one hundred homes every month in the Tri-State Area, with thousands of mezuzos being checked, fixed, and, if needed, replaced—over a thousand new ones are put up every year. The volunteers, members of the Crown Heights community, and Rabbi Kesselman make the effort to connect the homes they visit to local Chabad Houses.

Zalman continued to be personally involved in the organization throughout his life. In fact, he and Cyrel would go out once or twice a month to affix mezuzos together. "What better way to spend time with your wife than by going on Mivtzah Mezuzah?" Zalman would say.

Cyrel enjoyed the experience as well. "People were very receptive," she recalled. "It was great. You got out of the house, and you did a mitzvah. You always felt good when you came back home."

Zalman invariably took the opportunity to encourage the people he met in other areas of observance as well. He kept a notebook dedicated to these outings in which he would write down where he went and what happened. Often, the visits were learning opportunities for him as well.

Once, his son Mendy accompanied him to put up some mezuzos. It happened to be July 4th, and father and son found themselves in the middle of a raucous house party.

Zalman was obviously not happy to have his fourteen-year-old son witnessing the scene. "However, once we were at the home, my father knew that he had to do the 'work,'" Mendy said. The two went from room to room affixing mezuzos, doing their best to ignore the drunken teenagers around them.

As they travelled back home, Zalman told Mendy, "The Baal Shem Tov says that from everything you see, you have to learn something. From some things you learn what to do, and from others you learn what not to do. This was a lesson on what is not proper."

Years later, on a flight to Israel, Zalman was going up and down the aisles looking for someone with whom to put on tefillin, when one of the passengers stopped him. "I recognize you." It turned out that Zalman had put up mezuzos in the man's house some time before. Zalman noted that divine providence had clearly brought them together, and spent time talking with him about Yiddishkeit.

Packing up yom tov brochures to be mailed out.

Candle Lighting Campaign

Zalman also assisted the Rebbe's campaigns financially, giving to the International Campaign for Candle Lighting, headed by Mrs. Esther Sternberg.

He also gave generous donations to every shliach who approached him to help build a mikvah.

Zalman took an active role in building the mikvah in Amherst, Massachusetts, the Chabad House he helped found. Cyrel joined the committee of Taharas Hamishpacha International, and Zalman encouraged her activities there.

Lulov and Esrog Campaign

Though he always wanted to spend as much time in 770 with the Rebbe as possible, out of respect for his in-laws, Zalman would spend Pesach and Sukkos with them in Springfield, Massachusetts. He made the most of his time there, however, forming many acquaintances in the community, whom he encouraged to lead

Zalman with Jeffrey Kimball (center). Zalman's brother-in-law
Rabbi Sholom Tenenbaum is on the left.

more active Jewish lives.

Every year on Sukkos, Jeffrey Kimball, a lawyer and supporter of the Springfield Chabad activities, would host a large gathering in his sukkah. One year, the Edelmans arrived at the event without the Deitsches. Rabbi Edelman explained that they had gone to the local high school to look for Jews to shake the *lulov* and *esrog* with.

"When Zalman arrived he was very excited," Mr. Kimball recalled. "He told us that he was taken by the students' self-sacrifice to do the mitzvah." The lawyer was surprised. "Zalman, is this what you consider self-sacrifice? We're not in the Soviet Union. No one is going to be hauled off to the gulags for practicing Judaism."

Zalman explained that they had found only a few Jews in the school. Not satisfied, he had gone to the fields in the back and seen that the football team was practicing. He had turned to the coach and asked if it was okay for the Jewish players to make the blessing. The coach agreed, and with one whistle, he stopped the practice, announcing, "All Jews should go to the rabbi for a Jewish prayer service."

"Think about it," Zalman told those gathered in the lawyer's sukkah. "These are students who have little connection with their Jewish roots. It could be that there were some that never even told their friends that they are Jewish. And yet, in front of all of their non-Jewish friends, who may later laugh at them, they went to this bearded rabbi to say a blessing and shake a branch and a fruit. Is this not self-sacrifice?"

When Mr. Kimball retells the story, he adds, "I thought to myself that the one we have to be inspired by is my modest friend Zalman, who was always thinking about others."

On another occasion, Zalman was walking home from shul on yom tov in a very joyous mood, singing and turning somersaults. (Called "*kulehs*" by Chassidim, somersaults are an expression of intense joy. The upside-down position of the body indicates that joy has the power to reverse the natural order, and that a scholar and a simple person are on equal footing when it comes to joy because the feet, symbolizing action, are more important than the intellect.)

Along the way, Zalman passed a group of elderly Jews sitting in front of a building. To their great delight he did a few somersaults. "Did you ever see a Chassid make somersaults?" Zalman asked. They had not, they said. "It made our holiday!"

Pesach Campaign

His activities in Springfield expanded when, in 1986, the Rebbe encouraged people to make public *seders* for recent immigrants from the Soviet Union. Zalman immediately organized a seder for Russian immigrants in Springfield. Not only did he help fund the seder, but he also ran it with his children. For the first few years

Cyrel prepared all the food, and when it became larger, they had it catered. Once the Seder was completed, the Deitsch children would quickly organize the shul for davening the next day. ...

Afterward, the family would race to the Edelmans' for the family seder, singing nigunim during the two-mile walk home in the dark.

The public Seder continues until today, run by Rabbi Noach and Esther Kosofsky and Rabbi Chaim and Rochel Leah Kosofsky.

NO BUSINESS HERE

Zalman never discussed his business with his children. In fact, they say, when he came home from work, they could never tell if it had been a good day or not. All they knew was that he worked in *shmates* (the textile business). "He always came home in a good mood, ready to spend time studying with us," said Nechemia.

"In a way, my father's involvement in our future shlichus was already starting when I was growing up," said Shaya, director of Chabad in Montgomery County, Pennsylvania, "with the way he raised us with the ideology that we should become shluchim."

Toby recalled how her father would reverently repeat stories about shluchim. "He would give shluchim so much honor and respect whenever the family hosted them," she said. "You knew this is what he valued."

"He was dedicated to fulfilling the Rebbe's wishes, and that is

Zalman and Cyrel (sitting, center) with their children and grandchildren.

how he educated us," Nechemia explained. Zalman almost never took his children to the warehouse; they understood later that this may have been because he didn't want to spark their interest in the business. Toby once asked to go see the business, and Zalman responded, "*Achh,* what do you need it for?"

Zalman's plans for his children were evident to anyone who walked into the Deitsch home, Mr. Eagle said. "His true desire was in Yiddishkeit, *Chassidishkeit,* and being a shliach. That is where his true essence was. For the average person, it would be surprising that no one followed him into business, but he was not the average person."

Their rare visits to the warehouse usually occurred the night before Pesach so they could help search the building for *chametz.* Only after he married and moved to Fort Washington, Pennsylvania, did Shaya visit his father at work. "Perhaps it was because I had already found my mission as a shliach of the Rebbe."

Whenever his children consulted him for advice about their

shlichus, Zalman told them not to worry about their financial needs. "The most important thing is that you are fulfilling the Rebbe's mission."

In 2002, Levi and his wife, Miriam, were considering moving to Tysons Corner, Virginia. They travelled there to scout for a rental and test the waters in the Jewish community, which seemed ripe for a Chabad House. When Zalman heard that they had found a good location to live, but were not planning to move for several months, he was taken aback.

"If you have a place, move there immediately." Just as a child cannot learn to swim before he or she enters the water, he told them, they would not learn how to build a Chabad House without immersing themselves in the environment. "First you go and then you take care of the details." Levi and Miriam took his advice and moved two weeks later.

Before Rosh Hashanah, Levi was concerned that he wouldn't be able to gather a minyan for services, but his father told him not to worry. Even if only a few people came, it would be worthwhile. Levi advertised the High Holiday services and resolved to be happy with whatever turnout he got. To their shock, seventy people showed up, and things just got bigger from there.

Before Chanukah that year, one of Levi's friends offered him space in his office building. Encouraged by his early success, Levi made a Chanukah Wonderland. Some two thousand people participated in the activities over the eight days. The day after Chanukah, he spoke with his father and described the success of the event. Zalman just listened, and when he was done, asked, "What's next on the agenda?"

"I'm so tired I cannot think of the next project. I will consider it in a few days," Levi said.

But Zalman was not willing to accept even such a short period of inactivity. "You need to begin the next project today."

With Levi on his wedding day.

In addition to assisting other shluchim, Zalman began to help support his children who were on shlichus, but warned them never to become reliant on him. "If you want to grow, you cannot depend on my funding," he said. His lifetime of experience in the business world bore fruit in the advice he was able to provide as his children raised money for their Chabad Houses. Opening a Chabad House, like the beginning of any business deal, is always difficult, he told them. You just have to move forward until you see success.

Recalling the early days, when he spent much of his time collecting on accounts receivable, he warned them not to push off the difficult tasks in favor of the easier ones. "If you want to be successful, you need to use your energy for the more difficult tasks. The easier ones, pay someone else to do. It is well worth it, for in that time you could deal with the larger projects and grow the Chabad House activities spiritually and materially." Eventually, Shaya said, he no longer needed to rely on his father's financial support, but "I never gave up relying on his advice."

A piece of advice from his father that stayed with Nechemia was that if he brought people to the Rebbe, it would be easier for them to grow in observance. To this day, he encourages those who study for their bar mitzvah with him to be called up to the Torah at 770. "It's somewhat of a trip from Toronto," he said, noting that in addition to the

Zalman with Nechemia at the upshernish of his grandson at Chabad of Midtown in Toronto.

bar mitzvah boy's family, other community members often come along, "but the impression it leaves on them and their parents is unforgettable."

One family decided to send their son to a yeshiva in Crown Heights after his bar mitzvah at 770. The father visited once a month, and slowly became more observant himself. When the son came home for Pesach, he brought his father a present, a gartel.

Another sign of his father's influence on him, Nechemia said, is that he speaks about the coming of Moshiach during every class he gives, "even when the subject is not directly connected."

Just as the Rebbe had encouraged his father to send him good news, saying that it would bring him (the Rebbe) health (see page

79), Zalman urged his children to write regularly to the Rebbe with good tidings. After the Rebbe's stroke, as a young yeshiva student, Nechemia organized a group of people to call shluchim, from the Shluchim Office in Crown Heights, asking them to report good news to the Rebbe.

With his grandchildren.

Zalman often visited his children's Chabad Houses where, as in Springfield, he involved himself in the programming and developed relationships with community members. In Chandler, Arizona, he would hold farbrengens, telling Chassidic tales and singing nigunim. He always made a point of singing a favorite nigun, "*Volt Ich Hoben . . .*" attributed to Reb Mendel Horodoker. It is said that the Alter Rebbe would sing it as an expression of yearning for Reb Mendel, whom he considered his own mentor. Zalman would translate the words into English, explaining that it describes a Chassid's wish to be with his Rebbe:

> If I had wheels of gold, I would ride to you.
> If I had golden wings, I would fly to you.
> If I had a golden feather, I would write to you.
> If I had a golden ring, I would give it to you.
> Oy Rebbe! "Hark! My beloved is knocking: open for me,

my sister,
my beloved,
my dove, my
perfect one"
(Song of
Songs 5:2).

"He was suc-
cessful in giving
them a feeling for the
Chabad way," said
his son Mendy, the
shliach in Chandler,
adding that since his
father's passing he
has told stories in the
Chabad House, as his
father would do, on
Friday nights.

With Yossel (Jeff) Grunfeld.

Nechemia recalled how his father was constantly encouraging him to expand his activities in Toronto. "When are you opening a preschool?" he would ask. "And a day school?" In these last moments of *galus*, "we cannot become comfortable. We must constantly think of how to bring Moshiach closer."

"The locals loved to speak to him," Shaya said. "To them, a Chassidic businessman was an anomaly. If you were religious, you were a rabbi."

Zalman's lengthy Shabbos davening was particularly impressive to the Chabad House congregants, with some watching how he davened and listening to the nigunim he would sing during the service.

Someone once asked him what he was thinking about while he prayed. In reply, he offered one of his silent meditations: In

Dancing at the dedication of a new Torah.

one place in the service, we say that Dovid Hamelech gave Hashem a blessing. But how can we presume to compare ourselves to Dovid Hamelech? The answer, he explained, is that Moshiach will be born from Dovid Hamelech's offspring, and since we all have a spark of Moshiach within us, it gives us the right to praise G-d in this way as well, as Dovid Hamelech did.

Similarly, in the Shabbos davening, it says that everyone should rejoice over Shabbos just as Moshe rejoiced in the lot Hashem gave him. But how can our joy approach the level of a tzaddik's joy? Since every person has a spark of Moshe within them, Zalman explained, we can join him in his joy.

He made a point of greeting everyone in the shul, even those whom others tried to avoid, his children say. One congregant was blind, and many found it difficult to hold a conversation with him. "Somehow, our father found a way to speak to him for hours and to always share uplifting words."

A Home for Everyone

People who met Zalman and Cyrel at their children's Chabad

Riling up the crowd at one of his children's Chabad Houses.

Houses often ended up coming to Crown Heights and spending a Shabbos in the Deitsch home. The Lubavitch Youth Organization also regularly called asking them to host guests from out of town who would come for the Pegisha, a weekend retreat called "Encounter with Chabad" that brought nonobservant Jews to Crown Heights for a Chassidic experience.

Mr. Eagle, who was a college student in Amherst, remembered how, after his first visit, he was given an open invitation. "They were very warm and accepting of me."

As he became more observant, he faced some opposition from his family, and the Deitsch home became a refuge for him. "Even though they had a big family, I was like a son. I felt the love from him as though I was another son."

In fact, Zalman would say, "Here the Rebbe is the host," considering his home like a Chabad House, open to all. "There were always a lot of Shabbos guests; the table was always full," Mr. Eagle recalls. He remembers Zalman as a quiet but forceful presence. "He didn't waste words." Shabbos to Zalman "wasn't about him taking a rest or taking it easy, but just about doing the *avodah*."

This included leading the meal with words of Torah and song. "It was a very lively Shabbos table."

While he always welcomed guests, making them feel comfortable and included, he made a point of sitting with his children directly around him so that they were the center of attention. Though generally a reserved person, at the Shabbos table he would speak to every guest and ask them to share something from their lives, a story, or a meaningful idea they had recently heard or learned.

After every Shabbos meal Zalman would invite a guest to lead the bentching. He would also make sure that they would bentch over wine, a Chabad custom (*Hayom Yom,* 14 Kislev).

Zalman once asked Chaim Greisman, a dear friend of his son Levi and today a shliach in Stockholm, Sweden, to lead the bentching on Friday night. Chaim responded that the Rebbe had indicated that on Friday night, the host should lead the bentching. Zalman asked for a source, and Chaim pointed him to *Hamelech Bemisiboi* (vol. 1, p. 272).

The book chronicles some of the discussions that occurred during the meals that the Rebbe ate in the home of the Previous Rebbe on yom tov. On Simchas Torah day 5729 (1968), the Rebbe offered Rabbi Zalman Duchman, a well-known Chassid and chronicler of Chassidic stories, to lead the bentching on condition that he tell several stories. Rabbi Duchman told some stories about the Previous Rebbe. After a short discussion, the Rebbe passed the Kiddush cup while telling another guest at the meal, the Chicago philanthropist Yankel Katz, that he follows the Previous Rebbe's custom of only honoring someone else during the day meal.

Once Zalman saw that the Rebbe encouraged the custom, he immediately adopted the practice in their home.

Until today, the Deitsch home is known to be welcoming to guests. Cyrel continues to host many people to sleep and eat Shabbos meals.

BLESSED
HEIGHTS

I n the early twentieth century, Crown Heights was a popular neighborhood among Manhattan residents who wanted second homes over the relatively new Brooklyn Bridge. Stately brownstones were built along the tree-lined Eastern Parkway, and when the subway arrived, the neighborhood, which extends over a two-by-one mile area, became even more desirable.

By the mid-1920s, thousands of Jews lived in the neighborhood, which had some of the city's largest synagogues. On Shabbos and yom tov, crowds of people dressed in their holiday best strolled down the picturesque Eastern Parkway islands.

In 1940, the Previous Rebbe chose Crown Heights as Lubavitch World Headquarters. Chabad purchased a building on Eastern Parkway. The mansion soon became iconic, known simply by its address, 770. From there, the Previous Rebbe and the Rebbe reached out to world Jewry, directed Chabad activities, and

770 Eastern Parkway, Chabad-Lubavitch World Headquarters.

hosted world leaders.

A decade and a half later, however, Crown Heights was becoming less popular. Access to suburbs in outer Long Island by train and expressway encouraged more affluent residents to move out of the city entirely. The vacant real estate attracted lower-income buyers, who were mostly law-abiding people who lived peacefully side by side with their Jewish neighbors. Nevertheless, the Jews began to flee.

The Rebbe stood firm, refusing to abandon the place his father-in-law, the Previous Rebbe, had settled twenty years before. "There is no reason to panic," he told those who asked, writing in 1952, "People of color are decent people, and you can live with them peacefully" (*Igros Kodesh,* vol. 6, p. 299). Later, he would openly campaign and rally rabbinical figures to try to stop the flight.

White flight, as it was known, once begun, was difficult to stop, however, and as Jews continued to leave, the community gradually changed for the worse. By the 1960s, once-affluent areas had become, in several sections, dangerous slums. Real estate, businesses, shuls, and charities were the hardest hit. The elderly, many of whom did not have the resources to move, especially suffered.

The Rebbe beseeched (*Likutei Sichos*, vol. 6, pp. 350ff and *Sichos Kodesh* 5729, vol. 2, pp. 68–69): "Think not of yourself, but of your neighbors. Ask, 'What damage will I be causing them by leaving? What will happen to those who can't afford to move, or who don't have the strength to begin life anew?' Our sages said, 'Do not do to others that which you don't want done to you.'"

"*Kan tzivah Hashem es haberachah,*" became the Rebbe's rallying cry. Here (in Crown Heights), Hashem directed His blessing. In 1970, on the last day of Pesach, the Rebbe cited the Torah principle that the poor of the city should receive priority: "Therefore community members should support the local stores and businesses, which will then assist those who spend their time in Torah study, who will then work on strengthening the community."

All major events, the Rebbe said, should be held in Crown Heights. When Chadrei Torah Ohr, a network of afternoon schools and clubs in Israel, made their dinner in Crown Heights, the Rebbe wrote to thank them, "especially that it is being held in Crown Heights, where Hashem decreed blessing—to show to all nations that the Jewish nation is near to Him."

At the farbrengen the next week, the Rebbe said, "It is worthwhile for them to receive a special thank you that they are making the banquet here, in Crown Heights."

A few violent incidents sealed the larger community's fate, however, leaving the Rebbe and Chabad Chassidim almost alone in the neighborhood. Shuls were sold off one by one.

By the early 1970s, people's homes were worth less than their mortgages. During the Chanukah farbrengen in 1970

LUBAVITCH ARCHIVES

The Rebbe delivering a talk, 1971.

(*Toras Menachem* 5731, vol. 63, p. 26), after long talks on scholarly topics and the singing of nigunim, the Rebbe said that he wanted to discuss the situation in the neighborhood. There were those, the Rebbe said, who assumed that he had given up on the situation, because he had spoken about it only once recently.

"The truth is that this is not my personal issue. This is based on what it says in the Code of Jewish Law. . . . I am letting everyone know that it is false. I never went back on what I said, and I will not go back tomorrow or the next [day]."

The Rebbe then discussed a corporation, Chebro, which was established to purchase homes in order to stabilize real estate prices. Lacking funding, however, they were not successful. Soon, Chebro's homes were being foreclosed. The Rebbe emphasized that there was a need to let people know about the new initiative. He openly encouraged the community to purchase bonds, saying he would do so himself by giving dollar bills that would then be distributed to the other buyers.

Zalman and his friends, primarily Yitzchok Gurevitch, were deeply moved by the Rebbe's call to save the neighborhood. They invested huge sums of their personal money into purchasing homes and buildings. Over the years, the buildings filled up with Jewish families as the community began to grow again.

In 1976, the Deitsches purchased their home on Crown Street. It was considered a risky move, with only two Jewish families on the block at the time. When Cyrel raised her concern, during a private audience with the Rebbe, that her children would not have anyone to play with, the Rebbe replied with a smile, "Don't worry, there will be many children to play with." Indeed, within a short period, the block began to fill with Jewish families.

In the 1970s, the Rebbe asked that a hotel be established to host the thousands of guests who were flocking to Crown Heights. Immediately after Shabbos, Zalman approached the Crown Heights Jewish Community Council and said he was willing to supply half of the money to purchase a building for a hotel. By that Monday, they had already signed on a property on Eastern Parkway for that purpose.

In the winter of 1979, when Gershon Ber Jacobson, editor of the *Algemeiner Journal*, was planning a grand wedding for his daughter, he could not find a suitable venue and asked the Rebbe's permission to hold it outside of the neighborhood. G-d forbid, the Rebbe responded. "It would be contrary to all the efforts to strengthen the neighborhood, etc., especially when this is done by the editor of a newspaper." The Jacobsons ultimately built a tent in the courtyard of the Beth Rivkah school on Crown Street to host the wedding.

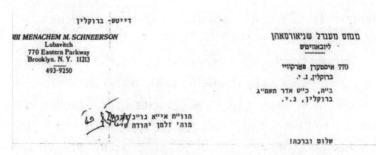

The Rebbe adds the title "activist for the needs of the community" before Zalman's name.

In 1983, Zalman received a letter from the Rebbe in which, next to his name, the Rebbe had added in his own handwriting, "*Osek betzarchei tzibur chulu* (activist for the needs of the community, etc.)." This, Zalman said, may well have been in honor of his work on behalf of Crown Heights.

By the late 1980s, after years of hard work and many ups and downs, the neighborhood enjoyed a renaissance beyond what Zalman and the many others who had fought for it in the 1970s could have imagined. Thanks to the Rebbe's foresight and their efforts, it became a thriving center of Jewish life.

LIVING
GEULAH

S tanding across from the Rebbe at farbrengens, Zalman witnessed the Rebbe's emotional, at times painful, pleas to his Chassidim to do everything in their power to bring Moshiach. Zalman saw that *Geulah* was the central goal toward which all of the Rebbe's campaigns were intended to lead, and likewise made it the centerpiece of his charitable activities and the focus of his life.

At the Shabbos table, he always looked for ways to connect the week's parsha to Moshiach and Geulah, and encouraged his children to do the same.

Every year, the family would gather together on yahrtzeits to learn Mishnayos and share words of inspiration. To find the correct chapters of Mishnah that would begin with the letters of the person's name, they would have to flip through many seforim. Once, a grandchild had the idea to make copies of the required

The Rebbe delivering a talk, 1992.

chapters that could be used each year. Zalman was not excited about the idea. "Moshiach is soon coming. All of our relatives will once again be with us," he said. "We will not need to learn any more Mishnayos in their memory."

In the years 5751–5752 (1991–1992), the Rebbe began an intense campaign to learn about Moshiach and Geulah in order to hasten its arrival. The Deitsch family, with Zalman in the lead, funded the printing of *Yemos HaMoshiach*, published in Hebrew and English by Tzach in Israel. The book was an easy-to-read digest of how the world will be when Moshiach comes.

Several years after Gimmel Tammuz, as the Kinus Hashluchim was approaching, Zalman wrote an open letter to the shluchim, whose ranks now included several of his children, with a cry from the depths of his soul:

> As Chassidim of the Rebbe our mission is to bring the Geulah in actuality, just as the Rebbe's goal was to hasten the coming of Moshiach.

Every year anew, when we prepare for the Kinus Hash-luchim, I pray and hope, and this is the feeling of each and every one of the shluchim and Chassidim, that by the end of the kinus, we will be with the Rebbe, and we should merit to see him again. The entire program and workshops are for one purpose: to find ways to hasten the coming of Moshiach and his actual revelation.

However, when the kinus is completed, and the shluchim return to their Chabad Houses, and we still did not mer-it Moshiach's coming, I feel that we have missed a great opportunity. This is a painful feeling, a feeling of "falling from a high roof into a deep pit" [Chagigah 5b].

I sit alone in my home after all of my friends and family who are shluchim have departed, and contemplate how it happened that another year passed, and we have still not reached the goal of the convention—the coming of Moshi-ach.

How could it be that thousands of shluchim sat together, learned, spoke, ate, and danced, however, the central part, the actual coming of Moshiach—they did not achieve?!

With all of the good discussions during the kinus, at the end of the day, this is not the only thing that is asked of them. The goal and purpose of the shluchim is to prepare the world to greet Moshiach. Therefore there needs to be a dedicated time during the kinus.

Zalman suggested that it be at the banquet, when all the at-tendees are gathered in one place. He proposed that it should include the saying of Tehillim, a talk about Moshiach, and, most importantly, to *shreyen mit a gevald* (cry out with anguish), "*Ad masei?* (Until when?)," to bring the actual revelation of Moshiach then and there.

The letter was printed in several publications. Whenever he

was with shluchim, Zalman would remind them that the reason they go on shlichus is to bring Moshiach.

What Will Be?

Throughout the painful period from the 27th of Adar I 5752 (1992), when the Rebbe suffered a stroke, until Gimmel Tammuz 5754 (1994), Zalman remained firm in his belief that the Rebbe would lead his Chassidim out of this bitter exile.

After the Rebbe's second stroke on 27 Adar I 5754 (1994) and his admittance into the Beth Israel Medical Center in Manhattan, Zalman joined the many Chassidim who traveled to the hospital each day to be close to the Rebbe and daven for his complete recovery. Often he was accompanied by his wife and mother.

He was once there very late at night, and one of the bochurim encouraged him to go home. "How can I go home when my father is hospitalized in such a situation?" Zalman replied.

After Gimmel Tammuz, his brother Avrohom Moshe asked him the painful question that many had at the time: "What will be now?"

The man who had gone through so much in his own family, and survived through his deep and unwavering faith, answered, "Now we need to strengthen our bitachon even more."

Zalman was referring to the time (see page 95) when his mother asked the Rebbe how she should pay the *shadchanus* money, to which the Rebbe responded, "If you strengthen your bitachon in Hashem, then you will be besimchah." The Rebbe then turned to all the family members present and said, "I am asking of you and your family to please strengthen your faith in Hashem."

This request from the Rebbe became Zalman's guide in every difficulty. After Gimmel Tammuz, he did everything in his power to strengthen the faith of his family and that of everyone he met. He also supported those who made it their mission to strengthen

The Rebbe leaves to the Ohel on 27 Adar I 5752.

Group photo of the International Shluchim Conference, 1997.

the belief of all the Chassidim.

Immediately after Gimmel Tammuz, Tzach, the Lubavitch youth organization in Israel, began to publish the weekly *Hiskashrus* booklet, which includes sichos, stories of the Rebbe, and Chabad customs for that week to strengthen the Chassidim's connection to the Rebbe. The Deitsch family has supported the booklet from its inception. Today, it is published by the Deitsch and Gopin families in memory of Zalman and his brother Yosef.

Zalman was known as a man of peace, but when it came to matters of faith, there was no compromising.

The day after Gimmel Tammuz, Rabbi Michoel Slavin had the idea that every hour, buses should go from Crown Heights to the Ohel. He did not want to charge for it, and he approached Zalman, who immediately agreed to assist.

When *Beis Moshiach* magazine began in 1994, with the mission to strengthen Chassidim in the belief and anticipation of the imminent coming of Moshiach and the Geulah, Zalman joined the board.

His children recalled that after the year of Gimmel Tammuz, he would occasionally come home with an uplifted feeling and tell them that he had experienced great success, more than he had anticipated, which could only be the result of the Rebbe's berachos. He would then quote what the Alter Rebbe writes in *Tanya* (*Igeres Hakodesh*, letter 27), that after the passing of a tzaddik, his presence is stronger than it was during his lifetime, because the *neshamah* is not confined to the limited body. He would then give the children money to buy seforim or something else they wanted.

[Part VII]

An Open Hand

KINDNESS TO A FAULT

The first decade of the twenty-first century was a dreadful time for the American textile industry. An agreement to end quotas on Chinese imports to the United States flooded the market with cheaper Chinese textiles. The effect on American manufacturers was devastating, "Free of Quota, China Textiles Flood the U.S." reported *The New York Times* on March 10, 2005. "In the first month . . . imports to the United States from China jumped about 75 percent."

The crisis reached Deitsch Textiles. However, the Deitsches had another calamity on their hands: Yosef, Zalman Deitsch's brother and crucial business partner, had been diagnosed with a terrible illness. His health had deteriorated to the point that he could not come to the office.

Faced with the unraveling of their business and an ill brother, Zalman encountered a new financial concern: How would he ful-

Zalman and Cyrel (sitting) with their siblings, partners in the business (left to right): Tsevia Gopin, Chani, Rishe, Avrohom Moshe, Yosef, and Gavriel Gopin.

fill his charitable obligations? It had been decades since the Rebbe had advised him to take over the family business, a directive he had obeyed despite having set his sights on being a shliach.

He had dedicated most of his profits to charity. "When the Rebbe sent me into the business world," he used to say, "I understood that my mission in life was to support the institutions and the activities of the Rebbe."

From the beginning, he brought a large check to the Rebbe's office each month, a significant portion of the company's profits. As the profits increased, so did the contributions. If he did not have the funds available to make the monthly commitment, he would borrow the money.

The Deitsch siblings and siblings-in-law followed his example and supported many causes, including Tzivos Hashem, Kollel Tiferes Z'keinim Levi Yitzchok, Machon Alte in Tzfas, Lubavitcher Yeshivah Academy in Springfield, Oholei Torah, and Tzeirei Agudas Chabad in Israel. They also contributed toward the extension of the Rebbe's library, the Heichel Menachem Library in Borough Park, and the building of the "1414" Lubavitch Yeshivah dormitory.

At Zalman's home, when collectors knocked on his door, he always invited them in and inquired about their well-being. His children said that when they saw their father sitting at the table with someone, they could not tell the difference between an old friend and someone who had just come to the door for a donation.

In 2005, however, Zalman was faced with a dilemma. Certain that his tzedakah was a conduit for blessings, it never occurred to him to cut back.

He turned to real estate attorney Donald Campbell of Bayonne, New Jersey. Mr. Campbell, or Don, as he liked to be called, had been his lawyer for several large building acquisitions in New Jersey, and the two had become dear friends. The lawyer said they shared a passion for G-d and religion.

"He was very warm, very engaging; [he was] intellectually open to discussion of how we saw our religious beliefs and [our] ability to handle the problems we saw in the world, work, and children," Mr. Campbell said. "Our business was secondary to our friendship."

Mr. Campbell knew that charitable causes were very important to his friend—Zalman had convinced him to donate toward several of them. He successfully arranged a loan; the terms, however, were extremely unfavorable to the businessman. The bank wanted, as collateral, not just the building Zalman had offered, but also the rest of his real estate holdings. They also wanted him to submit a solid plan for rebuilding his business to its previous healthy status. Zalman prepared one, which included investing more in real estate, and the bank gave him the loan.

He immediately began to distribute tzedakah in the merit of Yosef's recovery. This time, he decided, he would donate only to organizations that had no family connection. That meant that his father-in-law's yeshiva, his children's Chabad Houses, and any other family member who had an institution would not receive a contribution from these funds. "There is going to be no personal interest in this tzedakah," he said to his family.

The major benefactors were Crown Heights institutions: the Jewish Children's Museum, Mivtza Mezuzah, and Hachnosas Orchim (the organization that hosts the guests in Crown Heights for the month of Tishrei), and in Israel, Tzach, the Lubavitch Youth Organization, which heads Chabad's activities in the country.

His obligations met, Zalman began to look for real estate investments to revitalize his business. One major deal came via Mr. Campbell, who informed him that there was a large building for sale in Newark, New Jersey, that seemed like a good investment.

The property turned out to be difficult to manage, however. Many units were vacant, and the tenants were often behind in their rent. Zalman began traveling every day to Newark, where he hung up fliers about the building and spread the word among locals that it was under new management. His efforts bore fruit, and slowly, the building's financial health stabilized.

After Zalman and Yosef passed away, their brother-in-law Gavriel Gopin decided that the building Zalman had purchased in Newark was too far away from the family office for him to manage it effectively. It was decided to sell the property.

To the family, the profit from the sale was a final message from Zalman, assuring them that one never loses out by giving large amounts of tzedakah and that, in fact, Hashem would always repay much more than was given.

Chabad in Amherst

One of Zalman's first forays into supporting Chabad Houses was in Amherst, Massachusetts, the college town not far from Springfield, where his in-laws, Rabbi Dovid and Mrs. Leah Edelman, were the Chabad representatives and directors of the Lubavitch Yeshivah Academy.

Shortly after the Edelmans arrived in Massachusetts (in 1949/50), Rabbi Edelman began giving lectures on Jewish philosophy at Amherst College, a forty-five-minute drive from Springfield. For this class, which was based on the *Tanya*, the students received three credits. The Edelmans would also spend Shabbos in Amherst several times a year so that they could organize a minyan for students.

After Zalman and Cyrel got married, they spent many a Shabbos in Springfield, and when the Edelmans went to Amherst, they joined them. On one of these occasions, a student walked over to Zalman, who was then twenty-six, and asked if he could touch his beard. "I have never seen a religious businessman with a beard," he said.

This student turned out to be not just an undergraduate, but someone who already had a master's degree. Realizing how pervasive the lack of knowledge about Judaism was among the students, Zalman decided he would do something to help educate them.

"He schlepped twenty-nine students to our home," Rabbi Edelman recalled. "We sat with them the entire Shabbos, talked, and sang. . . . Whatever food we had was on the table." When it came time for maariv, the students had no idea what the prayer service was. "Characteristically, Zalman's response was to first dance with them."

That Shabbos in 1973, Zalman decided that Amherst needed a Chabad House. Shortly thereafter, he approached the Rebbe's chief secretary, Rabbi Chaim Mordechai Aizik Hodakov, and told him of his idea. "Who will fund the Chabad House?" Rabbi Hodakov asked. Zalman told him that he would fund it. "In that case," Rabbi Hodakov replied, "go into the kollel and find someone who fits the

Chabad of Amherst in Massachusetts.

bill for this shlichus position and then we will ask the Rebbe."

Zalman went to the kollel and asked around for a young man who would be able to work with college students. The top candidate was Rabbi Yisroel Deren, who was learning in Crown Heights after his marriage and preparing for a life of spreading Judaism "in a place where there are Jews, but not much Jewish life." He did not have a specific location in mind, however. "We knew that it would be wherever the Rebbe sends us," he said.

When Zalman approached Rabbi Deren about Amherst, at first he hesitated. He still had time to learn in the kollel, and he preferred to have an explicit instruction from the Rebbe rather than choose his own shlichus.

Around his birthday, he and his wife went into yechidus with the Rebbe. He asked the Rebbe where he should go on shlichus, and the Rebbe told him to discuss it with Rabbi Hodakov. He should also look into other locations, the Rebbe added. "When you have a list of places, send it in."

Rabbi Hodakov suggested Amherst, so Rabbi Deren wrote it down along with a few other options and submitted the list to the Rebbe. The Rebbe guided them to go to Amherst.

"From that day, Zalman supported us," Rabbi Deren said of his 1974 move. "He became our full-time partner in this shlichus. He also listened to our challenges and gave keen advice."

Zalman, then twenty-seven years old, took the Derens to Amherst to show them around, helped them find a home, and did whatever he could to make their move go smoothly. Later, the same year that he purchased a warehouse for the business, he helped with the down payment on the 77,000-dollar building for the Chabad House, paying the mortgage and supplying the Derens' salary for many years afterward.

Asked why he had done so much, he replied, "When I heard that the Rebbe wanted to establish more Chabad Houses, I didn't just want it to be the same support I would give others. Therefore I accepted upon myself to give the Derens their salary so they should be on sure financial grounds."

One day, Rabbi Deren decided to tell Zalman's mother about the support her son was giving toward the purchase of a new building and what they were accomplishing there. "How much is Zalman giving you?" she asked. When she heard the amount, she told him she would match it.

Over the years, Zalman had many different plans to expand the Chabad activities in Amherst. At one point, he wanted to open a kosher food store there, so Lubavitchers would move there and build up a proper community. Part of the profits, he stipulated, would go to the Chabad House.

He regularly visited Amherst to help out with the activities there. One year, he went to assist with the Yom Kippur activities and was also the *chazzan*. His young son Shaya was not used to the college scene. He recalled how he hid under his father's *tallis* for much of the twenty-four hours: "I was so scared that I even slept very close to him that night."

Whenever Zalman was in Amherst, the Derens would organize a farbrengen at the Chabad house so he could speak to the students; and whenever he felt it was appropriate, Rabbi Deren would send students to stay with the Deitsch family in Crown Heights, a Jewish experience they would long remember. Zalman also attended all of the Derens' family simchos.

"He was like our older brother," Rabbi Deren said. "He did not act like a boss. He would always tell me that the money was from his mother."

Rabbi Deren recalled that in 1980, his father had just passed away, and his brother was getting married in Israel. "I felt that since my father would not be there, I should go," he said. "However, for my wife, we could not afford [a ticket]."

When Zalman heard that Mrs. Deren would not be accompanying her husband to Israel, he wasn't pleased. He suggested that Rabbi Deren consult the Rebbe. Rabbi Deren wrote to the Rebbe, "Is it worthwhile that she should go?" The Rebbe placed a line through *is it*, making the sentence read: "It is worthwhile that she should go."

Zalman happily paid for the ticket, Rabbi Deren said.

In return for his generosity, Zalman asked only that the Derens use their time to the utmost. He once met Rabbi Deren in Crown Heights "on vacation" during the summer break and asked him, "Are there not enough Jews in the community [outside of the campus] for you to do activities with?"

Like many other shluchim, the Derens had their difficult moments. "We could always rely on him for emotional support," Rabbi Deren said. He recalled how, deeply upset about several issues, he and his wife once came to visit Zalman in Crown Heights. "He immediately recognized something was up." Zalman insisted that they go to a local restaurant. "Only there, over a good meal, did he encourage us to unload our issues."

Though Zalman demanded much of himself, "He had a sense of humor," Rabbi Deren said. "He knew what it was to extend a kind word with a smile. He was a warm man who always had a good word to say." After many years, Rabbi Deren eventually moved to Stamford, Connecticut, and today serves as the regional director of Chabad-Lubavitch of Western and Southern New England.

Today, the Amherst Chabad House is under the direction of Rabbi Chaim and Mrs. Yocheved Adelman and Rabbi Yoseph and Mrs. Zahava Gottlieb. With Zalman's support, in the mid-1990s the building was expanded and a mikvah was built, named for his mother, Mikvah Mirel. Over the years, many students were influenced by the shluchim and became baalei teshuvah. Some received semichah and others opened their own Chabad Houses.

Tzivos Hashem

In 1981, the Rebbe established Tzivos Hashem, "the Army of Hashem," an organization for Jewish children. The Rebbe felt that rather than fight against the often irreverent attitude of American youth, Tzivos Hashem should encourage acts of goodness and motivate children to strengthen their Jewish observance.

Zalman immediately joined the board. "His advice was worth its weight in gold," said executive director, Rabbi Yerachmiel Benjaminson. "He was blessed with good judgment, depth of understanding, and a lot of patience."

Zalman treated everyone he met with respect, appreciation, and dignity, Rabbi Benjaminson added, "Watching him was a life lesson." The organization knew that, in addition to his regular support, there was someone to turn to in times of need for loans or to give collateral for a loan.

LUBAVITCH ARCHIVES

The Jewish Children's Museum in Crown Heights.

When Tzivos Hashem built the Jewish Children's Museum in the late 2000s, the costs turned out to be four times the amount they originally budgeted, around $20 million. Rabbi Benjaminson heard that the Deitsch family's financial situation was not what it had been. "I understood that they would not be able to fulfill their commitment to the building fund. I decided that I would not pressure him or even bring it up in conversation."

He was surprised when one day Zalman asked him to come to his office. When he arrived, Zalman gave him a bank check. "Knowing his situation, my knees began to shake when I saw the huge amount," he said. "It was totally unexpected."

Seeing his reaction, Zalman told him, "Don't ask questions, use it in good health."

After the museum was built, all those who had helped fund it had a plaque with their names affixed on a wall. But Zalman requested that his name be immediately removed. The museum staff balked, however, arguing that it is "a mitzvah to publicize those who participate in a mitzvah" (see *Toras Menachem*, vol. 11, p. 21). In the end, they reached a compromise and put up a plaque in more general terms thanking the "Deitsch and Gopin Families" for their generous support.

Printing Tanyas

Zalman, in his regular reports to the Rebbe, included his contributions to tzedakah, and the Rebbe often responded with blessings for success in these endeavors.

On one of his trips to Nigeria for business, Zalman met a member of the National Assembly. He built a good relationship with him, and his business there flourished. At the same time, Zalman was thinking about printing a *Tanya* in the country. A year earlier, in Av 5738 (August 1978), the Rebbe had requested that a *Tanya* be printed in every country in the world. He wrote to the Rebbe asking if this directive also included printing a *Tanya* in Nigeria. "Even if there was one Jew there, it is worthwhile," the Rebbe responded. In 1979, after much effort, Zalman printed the *Tanya* in the Nigerian town of Aba.

In Teves 5744 (December 1983), the Rebbe asked that *Tanyas* be printed in every city where Jews lived. The Rebbe quoted the famous answer Moshiach gave to the Baal Shem Tov, that when your wellsprings (Chassidus) are spread to the outermost reaches, Moshiach will come.

The Rebbe explained that printing the *Tanya* everywhere

not only brings the "waters" of Chassidus to that location, but actually conveys the wellspring itself, which will surely bring Moshiach even closer.

After the Rebbe's talk, Zalman decided to rent a truck, place a printing press in the back, and pay for someone to drive it across the United States, printing a *Tanya* in every city.

He wrote to the Rebbe about the idea, and the Rebbe re-

The *Tanya* Zalman printed in Aba, Nigeria.

sponded that while it was a good idea, it would be preferable for the printing to be organized by the residents of the cities themselves. "It is better for the local community to fund the printing of the *Tanya* in their city. This way, the community will feel like it is their project and it is their *Tanya*," he wrote. Instead, the Rebbe asked Zalman to support several other projects.

Later, the project was resuscitated with the Rebbe's guidance. A mobile printing press was assembled, which could, at the request of a shliach, travel to any city in America to print a *Tanya*.

The Rebbe's Appreciation

Zalman and Cyrel once hosted a fundraiser for Chadrei Torah

A branch of the Chadrei Torah Ohr network of afternoon schools for Judaic studies.

Ohr, an organization that ran Hebrew school classes in Israel. It was customary for a bottle of l'chaim to be given to the Rebbe before such occasions. At the Shabbos farbrengen, the Rebbe would take the bottle and pour a little into his Kiddush cup, some into a cup for the person to say l'chaim and announce the details of the event, and give the rest of the bottle to be used at the fundraiser.

When it was announced that the event would be at the home of Zalman Deitsch, the Rebbe turned to Zalman and motioned for him to go up and take some of the l'chaim, a public acknowledgment of his kindness. "It should be with great success," the Rebbe told him.

Loan Savior

Crestfallen, a local Crown Heights resident was walking home from the bank after being told that his home was about to be foreclosed. He was out of work, and it had been a few months since he had made his last mortgage payment. The bank refused to wait

The Rebbe pours Levi (center) kos shel berachah.
Nechemia is on the right; Zalman is on the left.

any longer.

Zalman spotted the man as he stood waiting for a light to change. "I knew who he was," the man recalled. "But I had never met him, and I doubt he knew who I was."

Zalman asked him what was bothering him. Unable to restrain himself, the man spilled out his heart. Upon hearing what was going to happen to the family's home, Zalman immediately made arrangements to extend him a loan. "The walls of our home, I owe to Zalman Deitsch," the man said.

What the man did not know, said family members, is that in order to give him that loan, Zalman had to take out a loan himself.

The Gemach

Avrohom Moshe recalled how Zalman decided to open a *gemach*, a free loan fund, dedicated to the memory of their father, Sholom.

"He would receive many requests for loans," Avrohom Moshe said. "And he decided that it needed to be taken to the next level.

That was how he established the Keren Sholom fund." A board was formed, with Avrohom Moshe running the day-to-day operations. The process of granting loans would be transparent, with guarantors and payment plans.

In support of this new gemach, the Rebbe sent twenty dollars toward the fund, and they began to give out interest-free loans.

"But Zalman, with his soft heart, would from time to time instruct me to give loans without a guarantor to certain individuals," Avrohom Moshe said. "Soon, the Sholom Fund turned from a free loan society into a charity organization. Within a short while, there was nothing left in the fund."

Zalman himself was a guarantor for many loans from other funds. For example, the free loan fund run by the esteemed Chassid Rabbi Zalman Gurary was known to follow strict rules and only accept certain guarantors. Zalman was always accepted, however. In certain cases, when he knew that the person would not be able to pay back the loan, he would pay it back on his own even before the fund tried to collect the debt.

"Go, Go, Go"

In 1999, Rabbi Aaron Ginsburg established Chabad of Borough Park in Brooklyn. He wanted to have a proper board of directors, and approached Zalman, whom he had heard of but never met, asking him to join.

Soon, Zalman was an integral part of the organization, dedicating time, energy, and resources. Monthly board meetings took place in his home, and he began each with some words of Torah. "This was after a full day of work," Rabbi Ginsburg recalled. "He really heavily addressed many of the issues we had. Every meeting was another experience."

When it came to writing a mission statement, Zalman said that it should be about imbuing Chassidus into people's lives,

Zalman hosts a meeting of activists on behalf of Ezras Achim, an organization assisting Jews behind the Iron Curtain. Also seen: Rabbi Chaskel Besser (second from left), Rabbi Gedalia Korf (standing), and Rabbi Moshe Slonim (extreme right).

which would bring Moshiach closer.

He was levelheaded, Rabbi Ginsburg said, and at the same time he had an "underlying perspective that really imbued the entire organization and gave it a tremendous foundation. It gave me the understanding that we are working on a different frequency."

When it comes to the Rebbe's work, Zalman told him, you need to think long term. "His motto was, go, go, go." When they needed a second building, Zalman put his name on the mortgage.

Despite all this, said Rabbi Ginsburg, he acted as though his efforts were nothing special. "He never made you feel that you were imposing on him. It wasn't even possible to thank him for everything. He saw it as a privilege."

Competitor in the Family

After Yossel Mochkin married Cyrel's sister Zlati, he decided to go into business—textiles. "It was the same business as Zalman's," he said, "but on a much smaller scale." Yet Zalman never saw his brother-in-law as a competitor and helped him in any way he could.

"Zalman was an experienced businessman, and I was a beginner," Yossel explained. "He guided me through my blunders, taught me the basics of the business and how to purchase good quality fabrics at a good price."

In the beginning, Yossel was a young, "wild businessman." Zalman gently, but firmly, guided him on the correct path so that he would be able to support his family. When he struggled financially, Zalman would bail him out and signed as his guarantor on several loans.

Yossel recalled how he used to do mivtzoim in the middle of a work day and learn his daily shiurim. Seeing that his brother-in-law was easily distracted, Zalman told him not to mix his spiritual endeavors with his business. During your free time do mivtzoim and learn, he told him. "He understood the greatest tzedakah I could do was to bring a check home to support my family," Yossel said.

With Zalman, Yossel knew he could be himself. "He was my best friend," he said. "He knew my talents and my weaknesses. He always respected me and never disparaged my abilities."

TZEDAKAH
PARTNER

ttorney Jeffrey Kimball, a friend of Zalman's from Springfield, used to ask his advice before making an investment. Zalman would look at the details and give his opinion, but always concluded, "Jeffrey, you should know that the greatest investment is to give to tzedakah. From that you can never lose; there are only profits."

In 1985, the Machne Israel Development Fund began to hold a biannual conference, where philanthropists would pledge large amounts with the goal of supporting the activities and projects of the Rebbe and Chabad institutions. The climax of the conferences was a semi-private yechidus with the Rebbe. That year, during a lively farbrengen in his in-laws' sukkah, Zalman encouraged Mr. Kimball to join the conferences so that he could have a private audience with the Rebbe twice a year.

"How much do I need to contribute to the fund?" Mr. Kimball

Zalman (center) with a young Jeffrey Kimball (right) and Rabbi Yosef Gopin.

asked.

Since the fund was a new concept, Zalman did not know. "Say l'chaim, and pledge that you will give $950,000," he said, "and then you will be a partner in the fund."

"If I am already giving that amount, why not just make it a million?" Mr. Kimball asked.

"So that you won't go around boasting that you gave the Lubavitcher Rebbe a million dollars," Zalman replied.

The attorney pledged to give that amount, though it was far more than he could afford. In his weekly report to the Rebbe, Mr. Kimball notified the Rebbe about the pledge. Shortly after, the Rebbe's secretary, Rabbi Leibel Groner, called him and said that the Rebbe gave his blessing that he should indeed fulfill the pledge that he made in the sukkah.

Later, he became aware that the amount required to join the fund was $100,000, which could be given over three to five years. "However, since I had pledged much more," he said, "I decided

Rabbi Deren presents the Rebbe with the key to Chabad of Amherst.
Rabbi Dovid Edelman is in the center; Mr. Kimball is to his left.

that I would give that amount."

For years, in jest, Mr. Kimball would refer to the fund as the "950 Club."

Mr. Kimball became an integral part of the Chabad community in Springfield, and a major supporter of Rabbi Edelman. His charitable activities on behalf of the Springfield yeshiva in the city were a large part of his conversations with Zalman.

Once, the Springfield yeshiva was in a grave financial situation. The administration was unable to pay the teachers, and Mr. Kimball, a board member, did not feel comfortable. He called Zalman and told him, "I am sitting here, eating expensive steaks, and the teachers cannot purchase food. I am donating the amount needed to pay the salaries that are due."

Zalman was overjoyed and praised him for his generosity, but added, "Jeffrey, don't stop eating your expensive steaks. Continue to enjoy life."

In 1978, there was a fire at the school in Springfield, and

the entire building burned down. Rabbi Edelman believed that it was a good time to rebuild in a better part of the city, but had some doubts about the cost. "He was hesitant to take on such a huge financial responsibility," his son-in-law Yankel Goldstein said. "He thought that perhaps he should just rebuild on the current location."

Rabbi Edelman wrote to the Rebbe, who responded, "A new building in a new neighborhood."

The key presented to the Rebbe of the Chabad House in Amherst.

There was now no doubt what they would do. Zalman helped them purchase a new piece of land. As it turned out, there was no plumbing on the property. It would cost $160,000, a very large sum at the time, to install it before they even started building.

"Everyone was stumped with the situation," Yankel said. "My father-in-law had no way to come up with that amount of money." Mr. Kimball said he thought they should shelve the idea, sell the property, and use the money to rebuild the school elsewhere.

Rabbi Edelman would not make such a decision without consulting the Rebbe, however, and when he did, the response was

SHANA SURECK

Mr. Kimball with Rabbi Edelman at the rabbi's ninetieth birthday celebration, 2014.

The completed Lubavitcher Yeshiva Academy in Longmeadow.

that he should not sell the land. A devoted Chassid, Rabbi Edelman trusted that everything would turn out for the best and resolved to wait and see what happened.

Next door to the newly purchased property there was another empty lot, which was purchased soon afterward. When the buyer of the adjacent lot applied to install plumbing there, the inspector, who was an acquaintance of Rabbi Edelman and was aware of the situation, told him that he would give the permit on the condition that the plumbing was extended to the area, which included the plot next to his. The buyer readily agreed.

Today the Lubavitcher Yeshiva Academy, Springfield's Chabad day school, stands on that plot, built with generous support, among others, from Mr. Kimball and Zalman.

WELCOMING GUESTS

Zalman and Cyrel both came from open, welcoming homes and continued their parents' legacies on an even grander scale. Guests sometimes stayed for weeks at a time and were given to understand that they were welcome to return. Zalman did his best to make people feel comfortable by inquiring about their families and extended families until he found someone he knew.

One person described how he arrived in Crown Heights for the month of Tishrei 5752 (1991) with no place to stay. "I decided to take the taxi straight to the Deitsch home," he said. "When I arrived, I half asked, half informed them that I was there for Tishrei. With no questions, Mrs. Deitsch told me where to place my suitcase and a room where I could find a mattress."

The person said he was not the only one who "landed" that week at the Deitsches with no prior notice. "If I came back early in

With guests in the Deitsch sukkah.

the night, I slept on the mattress given to me. If I came a little late, someone was sleeping on my mattress, and I slept on a different mattress or on the floor."

There were people sleeping in every corner of the house, he said. The couple never required anything of their guests or asked when they would leave, but supplied them with whatever they needed. "There was only one thing that we all knew, not that it was requested directly," the person said. "When Zalman would come home and he would enter the library, it was our time to give him his peace and quiet so he should be able to learn."

While Cyrel encouraged her children to bring out-of-town guests to their Shabbos meals, Zalman too looked for people in shul who might not have a place to eat. Others, knowing that the Deitsch home was always open, made their way there on Shabbos without an invitation. Everyone around the table was invited to introduce themselves, say a dvar Torah, or begin a nigun. Many of these guests became like family. Cyrel kept in touch with them and invited them to family simchos for years afterward.

Each year, thousands of guests would arrive in Crown Heights to celebrate the Tishrei yomim tovim with the Rebbe. It was a huge logistical and financial undertaking to feed them and organize shiurim for all of them. The late Rabbi Moshe Yeruslavsky, who headed Chadrei Torah Ohr in Eretz Yisroel, took on the responsibility, and

With his cousin Nosson Kugel.

Zalman, who had a unique appreciation for the mitzvah of *hachnosas orchim*, was an important supporter of Rabbi Yeruslavsky's work.

After Gimmel Tammuz, the organization founded by Rabbi Yeruslavsky that arranges lodging and meals for visitors to Crown Heights was reestablished under the name Eshel Hachnasas Orchim ("Eshel"). Zalman joined its committee and convinced others to support it. Many thought that now fewer guests would come, but as the Chabad community around the world continued to grow, so did the number of guests who came for Tishrei.

Eventually, it became clear that Eshel, also a Hebrew acronym for "food, beverages, and sleep," would need a building of its own

Playing chess with David Schaffer in Springfield, Massachusetts.

to house the guests. They purchased a property on Kingston Avenue, but due to financial difficulties, they were not able to complete it for years. Throughout that time, Zalman helped them in any way he could. Today, the building is complete, housing many guests daily, with much of its success thanks to the Deitsch family.

The Deitsches' Tishrei hachnosas orchim reached a peak during Sukkos. After many years of spending the holiday with the Edelmans in Springfield, Zalman and Cyrel began to remain in Crown Heights for the week. Since they lived next to Kingston Avenue, they built a large sukkah and affixed a sign welcoming anyone in to have a drink and something to eat. Every night of the holiday there was a farbrengen in the sukkah.

Down the street from them was an apartment building where only a few Jewish families lived. The building managers were unaccommodating and for many years did not permit the building of a sukkah on their property. These families were always welcomed by the Deitsches to use their sukkah, and often simply joined the

Zalman and Cyrel host guests at their home.

family for their meals.

During one meal on Sukkos, Zalman went into the house to bring more food. When he returned and sat down, one of the guests approached him, saying, "Excuse me, but you are sitting in my place."

On another occasion, while Zalman was making sure that everyone had enough food, someone asked him, "Tell me, until when do you think I could remain here?" not realizing that he was the owner of the sukkah.

Zalman told him not to worry. "I have been staying here for a long time already, and no one ever asked me to leave."

His Needs

Zalman's consideration for others was legendary. Attending to his own needs, however, was a different story. He didn't enjoy shopping for himself, and on the few occasions when his wife was able to bring him to the store, he would tell her to buy several of everything that fit him so that he would not have to shop again for

Zalman during a trip to Israel, 1990.

a long time. Once, when his shoes wore out, he gave one of them to his children and asked them to bring it to the store and buy another of the same brand while he sat and learned at home.

When it came to the needs of others, however, he was thoughtful in the extreme. One daughter recalled how, when she was moving on shlichus, as the movers were putting the last things on the truck, her father disappeared and returned a few minutes later with coffee and fresh donuts for the movers.

Never Forgotten

FAITHFUL WEDDING

I t was mid-September of 1990, just a week before the Deitsches' oldest daughter, Toby, was to be married. The family was attending the wedding of one of their neighbor's children when, during the dancing, a commotion erupted on the men's side.

"We asked what happened, and we were told someone fainted," Toby recalled. "A few minutes later, we learned that the 'someone' was my father."

In fact, Zalman had experienced heart failure. When the medics were able to revive him, he walked out of the hall on his own, not wanting to disturb the wedding. At first, he refused to go to the hospital, but eventually, persuaded by his friend Avi Baitelman, he agreed, on the condition, in order to minimize the drama, that he would not take an ambulance.

At the hospital, the doctors quickly realized that he needed a

Reading the Rebbe's letter at a wedding.

full roster of tests and admitted him. Zalman turned to Toby and asked her not to be worried, and to go home and continue preparing for the wedding. She hesitated, he insisted, and eventually she went home with mixed feelings and a heavy heart.

As the days went by, worry sank in. Zalman's situation was not simple. The family was informed that he would need to be hospitalized for some time, and there was no guarantee that he would be released to attend the wedding.

"Someone like my father would not leave me to marry without him," Toby said. Indeed, on the day of the wedding, with the doctor's consent, Zalman got dressed and was driven to the wedding. A doctor attended the event to keep an eye on him, and though extremely weak, he participated in the ceremony and celebration wholeheartedly. When it was over, he returned to the hospital. The hospital would not release him to attend any of the sheva berachos, so one night, the family made the sheva berachos seuda right there in his hospital room, with one of the doctors serving as the *panim chadashos*.

Rosh Hashanah came and went, and still he had not been released. His brother Avrohom Moshe decided to stay with him for Yom Kippur. He was not permitted to remain in the ICU for long periods, but at the end of the day, during Neilah, the doctors let him go in.

In the Rebbe's minyan, it was the custom to sing "Napoleon's March" just before blowing the shofar to signal the end of the Yom Kippur services. The march had been played in 1812 by the armies of Napoleon during their invasion of Russia. According to Chabad tradition, the Alter Rebbe asked that the march be sung for him and designated it as a song of victory. Singing the march at the end of Yom Kippur is a sign of confidence that our prayers have prevailed and we are assured of a good new year.

In the hospital, when it came time to sing the march, Avrohom

Mr. Kimball asks the Rebbe for a blessing for Zalman.

Moshe stood on a chair and began to sing with great vigor, as was the Rebbe's custom. "Though Zalman was weak," he said, "I will never forget his wide smile and his happiness."

During his time in the hospital, Zalman asked his family to keep a positive attitude, as much for his benefit as for theirs. At least when they were with him, they made the effort to do so, especially Cyrel, who, with great inner strength, provided the support he needed.

Shortly after Rosh Hashanah, the Rebbe would meet with major donors of the Chabad-Lubavitch Machne Israel Development Fund to give them blessings for a sweet new year. Each donor was usually accompanied by the shliach from their hometown. The year that Zalman was in the hospital, Mr. Kimball, who would go with Rabbi Edelman and Rabbi Deren, requested a blessing for Zalman Deitsch's complete recovery.

The Rebbe asked how he knew Zalman. Mr. Kimball explained that his shliach, Rabbi Edelman, was Zalman's father-in-law, and he often came to visit. "I am very happy that you know

With his younger children: Chessy, Hindy, Rivky, Sruly, Rochel, and Nosson.

him and he knows you," the Rebbe said, adding that it was kind of him to think about Zalman's health. The Rebbe then said that next time Mr. Kimball visits, Zalman should already be well, "and if you will come ask something about him, it will be about healthy subjects." The Rebbe then gave him *lekach* (a piece of honey cake traditionally distributed before Yom Kippur for a sweet new year) to give to Zalman with a blessing for good tidings.

Slowing Down

Zalman was released from the hospital in time for Sukkos, but life did not quickly return to normal. Simple daily tasks became difficult for him. "My mother did not let my father leave the house alone," Toby said. The couple kept Zalman's situation to themselves and shared as little as possible with their children so as not to worry them.

Doctor's appointments became part of Zalman's routine. "I remember him waiting patiently in the waiting room, learning from a sefer," said Dr. Eli Rosen. When the doctors told him to stop saying l'chaim at farbrengens and smoking cigars, Zalman imme-

Zalman and Cyrel.

diately obeyed.

Even then, he was still caring for his younger siblings and their spouses. Before they could express their concern, Rishe Deitsch said, he called to reassure them that he had a treatment plan and everything was under control. "Doctors are not G-d," he told his family. "They know what they see, but Hashem sees beyond."

Zalman went back to work, and life continued this way for thirteen years, until Yosef became ill in 2003. Then Zalman dedicated his energy to caring for his brother Yosef and his children, once again trying to be a father to them all. He visited them regularly, walking from his home a few blocks away. Afterward, physically and emotionally drained, he sometimes asked one of his children to drive him home.

Around this time, he was learning a maamar from the Rebbe ("*Borei Niv Sefasayim*" 5748) with one of his children about how Hashem always creates the antidote before the sickness. Through Torah study, the Rebbe explained, one can access the cure for all illnesses before they arise. Zalman studied the maamar many times, and whenever he visited Yosef, he would repeat it out loud, even when his brother was unconscious.

Because Zalman carried on as if everything was normal, he was successful at keeping the extent of his own health problems hidden from the family. It happened that during this period, his brother-in-law Yossel Mochkin approached him for assistance with one of his children. Zalman made every effort to deal with the situation. "I had no clue how sick he was," Yossel said. "If I would only have known, I would not have had the chutzpah to ask."

School Improvement

Though he had been too busy to be involved with the school board when his children were young, during the last six years of his life, Zalman became an active member of the Oholei Torah steering committee.

Mr. Brook, a current board member who served on the committee with him, said that Zalman spent hours working toward solutions to improve the school. "He strongly believed that there should not be sweeping policy [of what was expected of a family] when it came to who could be accepted as a student. He believed that the best way to make change was to meet with families and encourage them to strive for a higher level of Chassidishkeit." If a child had to be removed from the school for various reasons, he made calls to other yeshivas and found one where he would be accepted.

Zalman devoted his heart and soul to the school, said Rabbi Yossel Rosenfeld, dean of Oholei Torah. "He had a keen understanding of chinuch. When he wanted to push something through that he believed in, he was adamant, and no matter how difficult it was, he would make it happen."

He recalled that there was once a board meeting a few days

The Rebbe's Ohel.

before Zalman was scheduled for a heart procedure. "I wasn't expecting him to come, but when I arrived, there he was at the table, as always, ready to share his ideas and suggestions."

Visits to the Ohel

After Gimmel Tammuz, visiting the Ohel became an important part of Zalman's weekly routine. Every Sunday he would prepare properly and study some of the Rebbe's teachings. Then he would meditate, replicating the feeling of awe with which he had entered the Rebbe's study in 770 on many occasions.

Writing his pan, he kept in mind what the Rebbe had told his father, "When I hear good news, I will be healthy." He would first report everything good that had happened that week and include the names of his children, nephews, and nieces from a list he always brought with him. At home, he never discussed his worries about the future, but to the Rebbe, he could open his heart, and he left the Ohel each week relieved and cheerful, certain that all his problems were now in good hands.

In an emotional 2006 speech, Zalman said that every time he visits the Ohel he thinks about the time when Moshiach will come and he will reunite with the Rebbe and once again dance with his entire family, including his parents and his deceased sisters. "I'll be dancing with all these people . . . *es vet zein* freilach [it is going to be joyous].

"I'm gonna be the happiest guy," he concluded. "Moshiach should come already, and we should be the happiest guys."

HOPING FOR
MIRACLES

By 2005, Zalman was being admitted to the hospital more and more frequently. It was becoming difficult to conceal the gravity of the situation from his children. Chessy recalled taking his father to the hospital for tests and waiting outside the room while the doctor examined him. Afterward he asked his father if everything was okay. "Everything is okay, with the help of Hashem," Zalman responded. "My father knew his prognosis," Chessy said, "but clearly did not want to pain me with the details."

Several months later, on Pesach, Chessy began to sense how ill his father was. They were in Springfield, as usual, but the forty-minute walk to shul had become an ordeal for Zalman. "On the way back, it was hard for him. It was then that it hit me."

That summer, Chessy went on Merkos Shlichus, visiting towns and cities across America that did not have established Jewish communities. At one point, his father's health worsened, and Chessy wanted to come home. But Zalman wouldn't let him, insisting that he had to finish his mission first. As soon as his shlichus was finished, Chessy rushed home.

Still, Zalman was optimistic about his situation. He liked to tell the story about Rabbi Chanina ben Dosa's daughter (Ta-anis 25a) who, after lighting her Shabbos lamps, suddenly real-

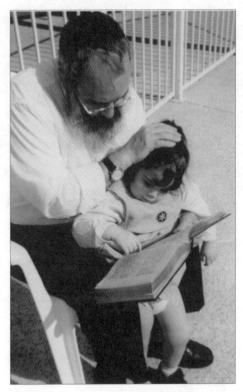

With one of his grandchildren.

ized that she had used vinegar instead of oil. Distressed, she came to her father to ask what should be done. "My child, the One who said that the oil should burn will tell the vinegar to burn," the sage responded. In fact, the vinegar burned until after Shabbos, when they used it for the Havdalah candle.

"The One who says that a healthy heart should sustain a person," Zalman would conclude, "could also tell an unhealthy heart to sustain a person." Chessy remembered how his father once found a sichah in which the Rebbe described the miracles that happened to the biblical Pinchas. "My father hoped that it was a hint that he would have miracles too."

Though he prayed for a miracle, Zalman did not neglect the

With Sruly (left) and Chessy.

medical means of healing at his disposal. He visited doctors regularly and, at their recommendation, registered himself for a high-risk procedure while being careful to keep these details from others.

Another Chance

The Shabbos before the procedure, Cyrel had planned a small Shabbos; only Zalman's brother Avrohom Moshe and his family would be joining them.

Rishe recalled that the two families had eaten together on that Shabbos the previous year and reminded Zalman what he had said about the parsha then. He seemed pleased that she remembered. He carried on a regular conversation and even delivered by heart the powerful maamar *Borei Niv Sefasayim* 5748 that he prepared in honor of his mother's yahrtzeit the next day.

In the poignant discourse, the Rebbe discusses how the process of teshuvah, return to Judaism, can happen in one moment, just as healing can sometimes happen instantaneously, with the right medicine. While food and drink have to be taken in abundance in order to nourish and sustain a person, "when it comes to medicine, even one drop has the strength to heal." Food does not have that concentrated strength, the Rebbe said, and "this is the strength of returning to Hashem, doing teshuvah, that it comes from a level that is higher than limitations and could happen in one moment." Teshuvah, the maamar goes on to explain, creates a new person, who is not confined by the same limitations and diagnoses that the person had before.

After the meal, Zalman recited *Shneim Mikrah V'echad Targum* and went to sleep.

The next day, Zalman and Chessy woke up early to daven. Zalman then opened a volume of *Igros Kodesh* of the Rebbe. Showing no signs of emotion, he said that he received a berachah. Then he, Cyrel, and Chessy took a bag with Zalman's basic needs and headed to the hospital.

Chessy and Cyrel studied the daily Chitas and Rambam with Zalman. Then they learned that week's Haftorah. Zalman explained that Yirmiyahu had been given a double mission. The first was to prophesy the destruction of the Beis Hamikdash, the second to comfort the people for their loss.

"These missions were difficult for Yirmiyahu," Zalman said. "They were not accepted easily, and those who didn't want to accept them made an effort to harm him. But Yirmiyahu was willing to place his life in jeopardy to fulfill his mission from Hashem." In the same way, he said, a Chassid must fulfill his mission, however difficult it may be.

Until the last moment, Zalman remained completely calm.

On Sunday, the family was called to fly in to New York to be with Zalman. Nosson, who was learning in London, arrived on Monday. After going to the Rebbe's Ohel, he came to the hospital.

The entire family gathered around Zalman's hospital bed and sang nigunim, their minds on the discourse, with a deep feeling of faith in Hashem "that our father would come out a new person" from his health crisis, as the maamar said, "in one moment."

Tragically, Zalman passed away on Monday night, the 29th of Tammuz 5766 (2006). On Tuesday morning, many people came to pay their final respects and escort him past 770, and from there to his resting place near the Rebbe's Ohel. A week later, his tombstone was erected. Knowing Zalman's dislike for titles, the family chose to have only those by which the Rebbe had addressed him etched on the stone: "*Osek betzarchei tzibur*" (activist for the needs of the community).

Zalman is survived by his wife, Cyrel, and their children: Toby and her husband, Rabbi Mendel Bernstein, directors of Chabad Romano Centre in Richmond Hill, Ontario; Rabbi Shaya and his wife, Devorah Leah, directors of Lubavitch of Montgomery County in Fort Washington, Pennsylvania; Rabbi Mendy and his wife, Shterna, directors of Chabad of the East Valley in Chandler, Arizona; Rabbi Nechemia and his wife, D'vora, directors of Chabad of Midtown in Toronto, Ontario; Altie and her husband, Rabbi Mendel Wolvovsky, directors of Sonoma County Chabad in S. Rosa, California; Rabbi Chessy and his wife, Laya, directors of Chabad of Tysons Center in Vienna, Virginia; Hindy and her husband, Rabbi Avraham Mintz, directors of Chabad of South Metro Denver in Lone Tree, Colorado; Rivky and her husband, Shimshon Vcherashansky, of Crown Heights; Rabbi Sruli and his wife, Mushka, directors of Chabad of Bronxville, New York; Rochel and her husband, Rabbi Levi Eisenberg, teacher and director of the Online Tutoring Institute; and his many grandchildren and great-grandchildren.

His fourth son, Levi, and his youngest, Nosson, passed away a few years later in 5770-5771 (2010) (see pages 260–279).

Playing ball with his children on Lag B'Omer, 1999.

LAST
MESSAGE

Attorney Jeffery Kimball felt that Zalman had sent him one last message before his passing. The lawyer called Zalman's cellphone while he was in the hospital the week before he passed away. Cyrel answered and said Zalman was resting. Mr. Kimball wished her husband a complete recovery and hung up.

Two minutes later, Zalman called back. In a weak voice, he said, "Jeffrey, do you think I forgot about you?" Mr. Kimball has no doubt that Zalman has not forgotten him. Certainly, he said, he can never forget the man who made such a deep impression on all who knew him.

After his passing, Zalman's family remembered his own response to the passing of his sister Rochel Leah Shusterman, in 1986. That tragedy had blindsided them, but Zalman remained strong in the belief that her life had been a full and meaningful one, which would inspire people for years to come.

"She was a music teacher, a regular teacher with so many students," he said on her twentieth yahrtzeit. "She was a great mother and a great wife." A strong Chassidic woman, yet very cultured, she and her husband had built a respected school, all this while she was in her thirties and already had eleven children.

With his granddaughter Mirel Wolvovsky.

He recalled how, soon after her passing, a business associate had visited him at work to offer his condolences. The man was young, unmarried, and wealthy. Zalman seized the opportunity to shake him out of his sense of complacency and urge him to get married.

He spoke with Rochel Leah's life very much on his mind. It was the first time he had spoken at length about his sister, Zalman said. "When you don't speak about it, you don't feel it so much. But when you say it . . . you feel it yourself; you feel it more." This is the reason we say the Shema so many times each day, he added, "because when you say it, you start to realize it more and more and more."

His sister's life had been a real one, he told the young man.

Zalman (sitting, right) with some of his children and grandchildren.

"You are alive, but is it truly living?" One can be alive, but spiritu-ally not. He quoted the *Tanya*. "You're still alive [because] you still have an effect on the world."

"It made a deep impression on him," Zalman recalled at Ro-chel Leah's yahrtzeit gathering, twenty years later. "He saw what life is all about."

Then he turned to his nephews with a message they never forgot: "Your mother, she did a phenomenal job when she was here raising you, and she did and is doing a phenomenal job sit-ting up there [in heaven]." Of course, it would be better if she were still here, "for all these good things should be done from down here." But, since that is tragically not the case, their mother above is thinking about them and giving them strength. It is their job to realize this, he said, and to honor her by using their lives in the fullest, most meaningful way possible.

Appendixes

PARTNER IN SUCCESS

Yosef Deitsch

Z alman's brother Yosef was born on the 23rd of Elul 1951, while his parents were in France. After the family moved to Crown Heights, he studied at the United Lubavitcher Yeshivah, afterward continuing his studies at the Lubavitch Yeshivah Newark and then in 770. In 1974, he married Chani Rosenfeld and joined the family business.

Zalman and his siblings shared a deep bond. They had gone through the tragedy of their father's early passing together, and together, they had rebuilt the family and the business to the point that they were able to donate significant funds to charities across the globe.

Yosef inherited his share of the famous Deitsch hospitality. Fully supported and encouraged by his wife, Chani, in addition to hosting many guests on Shabbos, they took in boarders, the children of shluchim who came to Crown Heights to attend school.

Yosef (center) with Avrohom Moshe and Gavriel Gopin.

When Yosef opened savings accounts for his children, he opened one for a young girl who was living with them at the time as well. Years later, when she got married, he gave her the money and the interest it had earned.

He was generous, not only with his material possessions, but with his heart. His children recalled how he would come home in a jubilant mood after hearing that someone else had a simchah, almost as if he did not distinguish between their joy and his own. He always made time to sit and talk with anyone who sought his counsel, and many Crown Heights residents found comfort in sharing their troubles with him.

Starting in 1982, together with his brothers and brother-in-law Gavriel Gopin, Yosef was one of the key supporters of Machon Alte, a seminary in Tzfas, Israel, named for his sister Alte Shula Schwartz, for women who have little or no prior Jewish education. Machon Alte students and alumnae knew they could stay with Yosef and Chani whenever they were in New York, and when they got married, they would often host their Shabbos Kallah and a

With the Rebbe on the 4th of Nissan (April 9), 1989.

sheva berachos.

The extent of their involvement became obvious when, six years after the seminary was founded, it needed a larger space. At the time, Chabad of Tzfas had a building that they were not using. The late Rabbi Leibel Kaplan, founder and director of the renewed community and institutions of Chabad-Lubavitch in Tzfas, had been Zalman's close friend and yeshiva study partner. He offered to sell the building to Machon Alte for the market value.

His brother-in-law Rabbi Yosef Rosenfeld, Machon Alte's founder and director, asked Yosef and Zalman for help. They, in turn, approached Chabad of Tzfas and requested that the building be given to the seminary for free, or at least a very reduced price. The brothers argued that Machon Alte was one of the Chabad institutions in the city, and there was no reason to charge them.

The shluchim to Tzfas disagreed. They needed the money the building would bring. They wrote to the Rebbe, who responded, quoting the verse in Bereishis (47:24), "You shall give a fifth to Pharaoh, and four parts shall be your own." The implication was

Machon Alte Seminary in Tzfas, Israel, named after Alta Shula Schwartz (nee Deitsch).

that Chabad of Tzfas should provide one fifth of the cost, and Machon Alte should pay the other four-fifths of the market value. The deal was sealed for $250,000, and over the next two and a half years, the Deitsch brothers made monthly payments toward the purchase of the building.

In addition to the seminary, Yosef was also one of the major supporters of Kollel Tiferes Z'keinim Levi Yitzchok for seniors (see page 110).

Another endeavor he was involved in was connected to his family history. During World War II, Yosef's father had been in a labor camp in Chelyabinsk, Russia. In an extraordinary turn of events, in 1996, after the fall of the Soviet Union, when Rabbi Meir Kirsh moved to Chelyabinsk and opened a Chabad House, Yosef paid for bochurim to fly there for Pesach.

Final Days

When Yosef became ill in 2003, he accepted his fate with love for Hashem, giving off an aura of faith throughout his harrowing treatment and making every effort that those around him should

LUBAVITCH ARCHIVES

Yosef (left) studying at a weekly shiur with Rabbi Avrohom Gerlitzky.

not know how much pain he was in.

Tragically, on the 8th of Av 5766 (2006), the day after the matzeiva was erected for Zalman, Yosef passed away at the young age of fifty-four, leaving the family and the greater Chabad community devastated by the double loss.

He is survived by his wife, Chani, and their children: Frumi and her husband, Rabbi Choni Marozov, directors of Chabad of S. Clarita Valley in Newhall, California; Rabbi Sholom Yeshaya and his wife, Chanah, directors of Chabad of Ridgefield, Connecticut; Altie and her husband, Rabbi Zalman Heller, the rosh yeshiva of Yeshiva Mesivta Menachem in Hastings-on-Hudson, New York; Tzippa Sara and her husband, Rabbi Mendel Rubashkin, directors of Chabad of Brandon in Valrico, Florida; Eliyohu and his wife, Rochel, of Crown Heights; Hindy and her husband, Shua Brook, director of family programs at the Aleph Institute; Chanochi and his wife, Mushki, of Crown Heights; and Mushky and her husband, Rabbi Eliezer Gurary, directors of Chabad of Chapman University in Orange, California.

THE JOYOUS RABBI

Levi Deitsch

Zalman and Cyrel's fifth child, Levi, was born on Purim Katan 5736 (February 1976). He spent his formative years studying at Oholei Torah Yeshivah in Crown Heights, where, his classmates remember, he had the unique ability to give everyone the feeling that he was their best friend. Each person Levi came in contact with felt "that he really cared for them and that they could always count on him," said childhood friend Rabbi Chaim Greisman, director of Chabad in Stockholm, Sweden.

"There was always something exciting. He would sing, crack jokes, motivate, and encourage. He knew how to give everyone around him the attention they needed and always had a good word for everyone."

New York City real estate developer Alfred Ohebshalom first met Levi when the young man, then thirteen, came to visit his

With his parents at the completing of a Torah for Chabad of Tysons Corner, 2005.

Manhattan office on a Friday afternoon. During what became a weekly meeting, Levi encouraged the businessman to put on tefillin and shared some ideas from the week's parsha. "His teachings were always filled with knowledge and the pearls of Torah," Mr. Ohebshalom says. "They were always rich in depth and meaning."

Levi was also an effective leader. As head counselor at Camp Gan Israel in Montreal, he worked to strengthen weak areas in a way that lasted long after his tenure. Seeing that the waiters in camp were not contributing to the Chassidic atmosphere, he singlehandedly changed the perception of the job so that it attracted a different kind of young person. "The Chassidishe bochurim felt that this job was not for them," said his brother Mendy. "Levi made this a most wanted Chassidishe position in camp." The change, intact until today, made a noticeable improvement.

After he finished his studies in beis midrash, he went on shlichus to Migdal Haemek, Israel, where he became a beloved mentor to the students in the yeshiva. He taught them many nigunim they had not heard before, one of which became a favorite of the students. When the bochurim were in New York for Tishrei, some were guests at the Deitsch home for Shabbos. When Zalman asked them to say a dvar Torah or sing a nigun, they immediately began to sing what they called "Levi's Nigun." From then on, Zalman referred to it by that name with pride.

In 2001, Levi married Miriam Loebenstein from Melbourne, Australia. A year later, the couple moved to Vienna, Virginia, where they started the Chabad of Tysons Corner.

When Levi and Miriam told Mr. Ohebshalom that they were going to move to Virginia to open a Chabad House, he was taken aback. "I had no idea that a young man of his age was capable of achieving precisely that." On further reflection, however, he realized that there was no reason the couple shouldn't succeed. "Because of his charisma and inborn love of Hashem, it seemed as if he could truly do anything."

In Virginia, Levi's people skills proved invaluable. "He was a friend to everyone," said Glenn Taubman, a community member, "with a smile and a laugh that never quit. He was a sweet and gentle guy, a real mentsch in every sense of the word."

Bonnie Wald-Jawer first met Levi at a Chanukah Wonderland event in Vienna. "We were struck by his energy, his charm, and the sheer enthusiasm of his welcome." Community members recall how he went out of his way to make people feel comfortable. Those who struggled to find their place in the community got extra personal attention from the rabbi.

Aware that many people were hesitant to attend religious events, he made a grand Lag B'Omer barbeque each year, and invited those who didn't come to shul. When one man declined, saying he wasn't interested in observance, Levi pulled him aside. "In order to fulfill the mitzvah of Lag B'Omer," he said seriously, "you need to have a lot of hotdogs, chips, and soda."

Slowly, the community began to grow. Drawn by the young

rabbi's enthusiasm, once-a-year Jews became weekly regulars; attendance at Torah classes increased. "He is responsible for many people reaching new heights of learning and Yiddishkeit," Mr. Taubman said.

Levi's memory and attention to detail impressed many of the congregants with the feeling that he really cared. A man who never attended Torah classes was taken by surprise when Levi, unprompted, dedicated a class in honor of his mother's yahrtzeit. "How could I not attend?" he said, noting that the class sparked his interest in Yiddishkeit.

He was a "joyous man, a joyous rabbi, a joyous husband and father," said Len Levine, recalling that Levi would find a way to bring joy "even to the most serious of subjects."

To people who told him they weren't Orthodox, he would joke, "Do you know why we are supposed to be buried six feet down? Because 'deep down' we are all good Jews." To others he would say, "Do not confuse Jews with Jewish observance, and love everybody."

As families became more observant, Levi helped them navigate sticky situations. The son of one family he had nurtured decided to attend yeshiva, and returned home full of what he had learned. He made a comment in shul to his father about something he was doing wrong, and Levi, overhearing the exchange, took him aside. "Your father brought you into this world," he said. "Even if you know more than him, it is not your place to publicly correct him."

When another family was struggling to reconcile their differences over Yiddishkeit, Levi told them to look for the positive in every situation. "Saying 'no' to the other's request is easy," he told one spouse. "Any rabbi can say no, but a good rabbi will try to find a way to say yes." The advice, the spouse said later, "allowed me to avoid a possible family rupture and keep peace."

At his son Zalman's upshernish.

When needed, Levi would aid people financially. "He was always there for me, helping to get my life straight," said Dr. Stanko Petrov, "buying my undergrad books, bringing food when I was sick, going out [of his way] to cheer me up, and talking about life."

Levi was very organized with the Chabad House finances, and often said that public money should be spent with the utmost transparency and accountability. He would also give loans to his friends and fellow shluchim. When one friend asked for a large loan, Levi readily agreed, but told him, "Someone like you should not need to take a loan. With your talents, you should be the one giving loans." Today, this friend helps others with loans.

After his father's passing, Levi began to learn with Rabbi Greisman in Sweden over the phone. Over time, others joined the weekly call. "The shiur was very dear to Levi, and he would make every effort to join," Rabbi Greisman said.

In 2007, at the age of thirty-one, Levi was diagnosed with

Celebrating the completion of a new Torah.

lung cancer. Ignoring the doctors' grave predictions, he began a war against all odds to continue his work, with the motto of the Tzemach Tzedek (*Sefer Hamaamarim* 5687, p. 236), "Think good and it will be good," ringing in his ears.

Soon, however, the treatment plans and medical decisions began to pile up, and Levi realized he would need help. Every Rosh Hashanah and Yom Kippur, Dr. Donald Infeld, a specialist in internal and emergency medicine, would join the Chabad House davening. Levi didn't know the doctor well, but he instinctively turned to him for support.

"I love the way you conduct your minyan. I will be here to help you with whatever you need," the doctor said, offering to help Levi navigate the medical system. Shortly thereafter he made the first of many visits to the Deitsch home.

"Rabbi Levi was a five-star general preparing for what he knew would be a protracted and difficult war against a tough and unrelenting enemy," Dr. Infeld said. "Yet, to his last breath, he was absolutely certain that he would beat this illness, and the prospect of having a medically knowledgeable and connected aide-de-camp at his side was extremely appealing. He embraced my offer and, indeed, he embraced me."

Indeed, Levi was overjoyed to be able to fulfill the Rebbe's frequently repeated advice to consult a doctor "who is a friend." He told friends and family that he knew Dr. Infeld was well qualified in both areas.

At first, Levi kept the details of his illness from his community, worried that people would stop coming to him with their burdens. One community member later said that he was shocked to learn that the rabbi, who had given him much-needed encouragement during his own bout with cancer, had been ill himself at the same time. Throughout, Mr. Ohebshalom said, "Levi still carried his famous smile and approached all issues of life with a positive attitude."

When Levi was in the hospital for treatment, friends, family, and shluchim from across the globe came in to visit. Dr. Infeld, who during the most difficult periods in his treatment spent whole days and nights with the rabbi, said he never knew that such love and care for a friend existed. "On numerous occasions, his ward at NIH [the National Cancer Institute, a division of National Institutes of Health (NIH) in Bethesda, Maryland] looked like the streets of Crown Heights on a spring Sunday."

Despite his pain, Levi was a fountain of faith, encouraging his visitors not to feel depressed about his situation. "His emunah in Hashem, his love of humanity, and his outstanding character never faltered," Mr. Ohebshalom said. "It was precisely these virtues that carried him so long and helped him overcome all of the obstacles."

When Levi finally made his illness public, a naturopath tried to help him with alternative medicine. After six months, Levi decided to also do chemotherapy. When this person found out, he was insulted and cut off ties with the rabbi. Yet Levi, as usual, con-

Giving a class.

tinued to call the man every Friday to wish him good Shabbos, even if his calls were not taken.

One day Levi learned that this person's son was a masseur, and practiced in the same location as his father. He immediately made an appointment for a massage in an effort to heal the rift that had opened between them. Sadly, Levi was hospitalized a day before the appointment and was unable to keep it.

At one point, several doctors came to tell him that it was time for him to prepare a will and say goodbye to his family and community. Levi became very serious. "Are you guys with me or against me?"

For the next twenty minutes, as the doctors kneeled by his bedside to be eye level with him, he explained that if they were there to help him, cared about him, and believed that he had a chance, they had to continue to look for ways to assist him to overcome his illness. "If this is true, great. Otherwise I have nothing to do here at this hospital." He reminded them that a doctor needs to believe in G-d, who gives strength, life, and blessings to do what

Always with a smile and a warm embrace.

is right, and be the messenger who bestows the blessing of health, "otherwise, I'm leaving immediately."

From that day on, the doctors made an effort to adopt a positive attitude. One of the doctors even came to visit on his day off.

As the Kinus Hashluchim of the year 5771 (2010) approached, friends who were coming to New York from across the globe made an effort to visit Levi in the hospital in Maryland. "It was very obvious that his condition was not good," said Rabbi Greisman. "Nevertheless, he made an effort to joke around and talk about whatever, as if all was well."

His friends saw that though he was getting weaker, the spark in his eyes was not dimmed. "I will win," he said, lifting his fist into the air.

At the international conference's Motzei Shabbos *Melave Malka*, thousands of shluchim sang the soul-stirring nigun of Reb Michel of Zlotchov together in his merit, as Levi watched on a live feed. The melody was very dear to the Baal Shem Tov, who said that it arouses great mercy (*Sefer Hanigunim* vol. 1, p. XLVIII).

Riling up the crowd at a Purim celebration.

During the actual kinus, his brother Rabbi Shaya and brother-in-law Rabbi Mendel Wolvovsky decided to make a farbrengen with Levi in his hospital room. Realizing they had no l'chaim, they approached one of the doctors, who wrote them a prescription for vodka, usually prescribed for alcoholics who are dealing with dangerous effects from total withdrawal. At the mini-farbrengen, they told stories and shared words of encouragement. Levi asked them to sing only joyous nigunim.

A week later, on Shabbos afternoon, the sixth of Kislev 5771 (November 13, 2010), Levi passed away. He was thirty-four years old.

During the *shiva* and shloshim, hundreds came to comfort the family and community. All struggled to accept the fact that their rabbi and friend was no longer with them. Many people penned their memories, which were posted, and can still be read, at RabbiLevi.com.

ENERGETIC SCHOLAR

Nosson Nota Deitsch

Zalman and Cyrel's youngest child, Nosson, was born on Shabbos, the 19th of Sivan 5748 (1988). He was named after his great uncle Rabbi Nosson Nuta Zuber, who had been a student at the original Tomchei Temimim yeshiva in the town of Lubavitch, Russia. Fluent in the entire Tanach at the age of eight, and later in the entire Talmud, Rabbi Zuber eventually immigrated to the United States and served for six decades as the rabbi at the Beth David Synagogue in Roselle, New Jersey.

His namesake followed in his footsteps, displaying an interest in study at an early age. When he was four, Nosson awoke one night to hear family members hastily preparing to leave the house. The Rebbe was distributing a booklet of the maamar *"Vikibeil Hayehudim."* Nosson begged to join them, and was given permission. He treasured his copy of the maamar, which turned out to be,

as of now, the last time the Rebbe distributed a booklet.

Nosson studied at Oholei Torah, then at the Mesivta of Staten Island (located today in Westchester), headed by his cousin Rabbi Zalman Heller. He continued his studies in England; then in Kiryat Gat, Israel; Los Angeles, California; and later in Miami, Florida. He was known as a diligent student who frequently would retreat to a quiet corner to study, often learning the material by heart.

Before his bar mitzvah, his parents hired someone to study the bar mitzvah maamar with him, but after three lessons, the tutor said there was no reason for him to continue. "I have never had such a successful student."

The Rebbe gives Nosson, in his mother's arms, a dollar to give to tzedakah.

At the age of twelve, he studied the first twelve chapters of *Tanya* and learned them by heart. As a reward, he spent Shavuos at the Chabad House of his brother Mendy and sister-in-law Shterna, in Chandler, Arizona. "The visit of a young boy who knew so much Torah by heart," Mendy recalled, "made a huge impression upon the community."

At his bar mitzvah, he not only recited the maamar, but did so with much vigor and delight.

Later, at the encouragement of his father and with much effort, he would learn by heart all fifty-three chapters of the *Tanya* and the twelve chapters of *Igeres Hateshuvah* as well. To keep them fresh in his mind, he had a system where he would review a certain amount each day. At least once a month, he would review all sixty-five chapters by heart. In one of his *Tanyas*, he wrote that he had reviewed by heart the entire *Igeres Hateshuvah* in forty-two minutes.

In camp one year, he and one of his cousins held a competition to see who would be able to study more material by heart. At

With Zalman.

the end of the summer, they both returned home with the many seforim they had received as prizes for their achievements.

Nosson already possessed an impressive library. Some volumes he purchased with his own money, others he received as prizes for excelling in his studies. Even when he won money, he would use much of it to buy books. Always pushing himself to achieve more, he could already be heard at six in the morning studying out loud. In the evenings, his family often found him surrounded by seforim, writing notes in the margins.

Like his father and siblings, Nosson was a people person who made an effort to befriend his classmates, even those whom others did not befriend. One classmate had an unpleasant odor and was consequently avoided by the other boys, but Nosson made a point of sitting next to him.

A friend who asked for a favor, even on short notice, was never refused. For an entire year, Nosson tutored one friend who was having trouble learning a maamar, giving him the tools to be able to study on his own. Another, who had little interest in continuing

Nosson receives a prize of seforim for studying Mishnah by heart.

his studies, he persuaded to study the *Hayom Yom* each day with him. If his friend did not have the sefer, he would send him the day's entry via text message.

Constantly on the lookout for a new study regimen and partner, Nosson studied Shulchan Aruch each day with a person who had recently become observant. After the tragic passing of Shula Swerdlov, the young daughter of his cousin, who was hit by a bus in 2009 in Yerushalayim, he began to learn part of a maamar of the Previous Rebbe each day in her memory. Unbeknownst to his family, Nosson contributed $500 toward the Torah written in her memory.

He also influenced his nieces and nephews to follow his example, offering them prizes for studying *Tanya* by heart. At the age of ten, he was already purchasing *siddurim* for them, many times adding a note in each one to specify what had been done to earn it.

As befit a serious student, he was disciplined in all areas of his life and followed his father's example in going to bed at a timely hour, even when there was a lot of commotion in the house,

Dancing during "*Haneiros Halalu*" with (left to right) Rochel, Zalman, Nosson, and Rivky.

so that he could wake up early (usually 6 a.m.) and study with a clear head. Family members recalled waking up to the sound of his voice studying Torah.

During his time off from yeshiva, he traveled to shluchim across the United States to assist them. After one such engagement, a community member turned to the shliach. "Can you bring this young Chabad student more often? He is so joyous, genuine, and sweet. There is so much to learn from him."

One Chanukah, he was helping a shliach at his large menorah lighting event when it began to pour, and people started to head for their cars before the program began. Nosson suggested that the shliach should have the musicians play energetic music, then he grabbed several people by the hand and began to dance. Many on the sidelines joined in and, since they were already wet, stayed for the lighting as well.

His friends often joined him in organizing an event at a Chabad House. They were never surprised when he would point to an office building en route and say, "Come, let's check to see if there is anyone in the building we could put on tefillin with."

Another of Nosson's weekly rituals was to write a pan and send it to the Rebbe's Ohel.

When his brother Levi became ill, he began traveling to Virginia often to help out. Nothing was too difficult for him to do—he would schlep tables, set them up, put on tefillin with community members, give a talk, lead a class, or sing and dance with the group.

As soon as he had some money, he would give a portion of it away to tzedakah, often to his siblings on shlichus.

While studying for semichah in Miami, Nosson jumped at the chance to help out at the Lag B'Omer parade in Valrico, Florida, where his cousins Rabbi Mendel and Tzippy Rubashkin are co-directors of the Chabad Jewish Discovery Center. He and several other students received permission to go from the yeshiva, and they were of great assistance at the event. During that day, Nosson was in an accident that, to his friends and family's painful shock, took his life. He was only twenty-one years old.

At the time, he was in the midst of learning by heart the twelve chapters of *Shaar Hayichud Vehaemunah*, which, among other things, discusses that G-d's ways are beyond our understanding and that only good comes from Hashem.

With much grief, the family sat shiva in Crown Heights, where they received a constant stream of visitors. His brother Levi, despite his failing health and constant pain, greeted everyone with a smile. His friends said that *he* was the one who consoled them.

Seven days later, family members gathered at the Ohel, quietly reciting Tehillim before they would erect the matzeiva for Nosson. His great-aunt Mrs. Chana Sharfstein recalled the solemn mood. "Each mourner deep in thought of the young man who had suddenly been taken from us."

As they stood in the Ohel after reading a general pan from

the family, the silence was broken with a nigun. The other brothers joined in, and the singing grew louder. "Tears began to stream down my face as the six brothers continued their singing," Mrs. Sharfstein wrote. "Their hearts were broken, yet they proclaimed their unwavering faith in the Almighty. I thought of Jewish heroes of the past: Marranos approaching the tribunal of the Inquisition; Ho-

On mivtzoim in a mall.

locaust victims walking to the gas chambers or trudging down dark, dreary roads on a death march, loudly chanting the prayer of Shema or singing 'Ani Maamin,' their faith never faltering. The historic scenes of the past were now reenacted by the brothers. It was an unforgettable experience."

Tributes to Nosson and memories treasured by his family and friends can be found at RememberingNosson.com.

MEMORIES OF MY CHILDHOOD

By Reb Mendel Deitsch—Zalman Deitsch's grandfather

Zalman's grandfather Reb Menachem Mendel Deitsch was born in 1882 in the town of Dokshitz, Belarus, to Reb Yosef (son of the famed Reb Yekusiel of Dokshitz) and Chana Devorah (daughter of Reb Yisroel Ber Rubin of Velizh, a Chassid of the Tzemach Tzedek and Rebbe Maharash). He had two siblings, Shmuel and Alte Shula (mother of Mirel Deitsch). He also had three half-siblings from his father's second marriage, Zalman Isser "Sol," Monne "Manuel," and Nochum "Norman" Deitz.

In his memoirs, written in Yiddish, a portion of which is translated and adapted here, he describes the town of Dokshitz, where he grew up and lived for a period after his marriage.

My paternal grandfather, Reb Yekusiel Deitsch, whom everyone called "Kushe Dokshitzer," was well-known in the world of Lubavitch Chassidim [and is mentioned in several talks of the Rebbe Rayatz (see, for example, *Sefer Hasichos* 5696–*Choref* 5700, p. 198 and the footnote there)].

As a young man, he was a Chassid of the Tzemach Tzedek; in midlife, after the passing of the Tzemach Tzedek, he became a disciple of the Rebbe Maharash; and in his last years, a devoted follower of the Rebbe Rashab, though he had known the Rashab from the age of three.

For five decades, my grandfather would go to Lubavitch for the month of Tishrei every year, usually traveling [the 160 miles] on foot. In addition, he made several unplanned visits to the Rebbe during the year—upon leaving the study hall, he would simply start walking toward Lubavitch rather than return home.

Spending Tishrei in Lubavitch provided Reb Yekusiel with spiritual "food" for the entire year, infusing new life into his davening and study of Chassidus. His time with the Rebbe also replenished his arsenal of Chassidic wisdom, which he used to influence his fellow townsmen, many of whom became connected to Chabad-Lubavitch through him.

Below are some memories of Zeide Yekusiel's devotion to the Rebbe Rashab:

The Yellow Cream

When one of his daughters [my aunt] became sick and lost her eyesight, Grandfather immediately set out to Lubavitch and asked the Rebbe Rashab what to do. "In your town of Dokshitz lives an apothecary, Berel Moshe Shmotkin," the Rebbe said. "Ask him for the yellow cream and smear it on her eyes."

Grandfather went to Berel Moshe and repeated the Rebbe's

The center of Dokshitz.

directive.

A devoted Chassid of the Rebbe himself, the apothecary tried hard, but could not recall having yellow cream in stock. "I have only white cream," he said.

"Make it yellow," Grandfather urged.

Berel Moshe added something to the cream that made it yellow; Reb Yekusiel quickly went home, smeared it on his daughter's eyes, and she recovered her sight.

From then on, anyone in Dokshitz who had problems with their eyes would come to Grandfather. He would give them some of the yellow cream, and they would be healed.

Which World Are You In?

My grandfather's dear friend Reb Aaron "Oreh Dokshitzer," a grain merchant, sometimes accompanied him on his trips to Lubavitch.

Oreh's business was to purchase grain from local farms and smaller merchants and send it to the city of Smorgon. At the time, there were no train stations near Dokshitz, so he sent the grain by wagon.

On the day of the shipment, he would hire locals to help him gather the grain and bring it to a central location. They made quite a procession: Oreh in front with a shining face, obviously contemplating a maamar Chassidus, and behind him a train of men pulling handcarts laden with grain.

Oreh lived next to the Berezina River in an area called Sloboda. Every Shabbos we would go to his home to hear a maamar. Most of the Chassidic farbrengens in Dokshitz were in his home, including the grand feast for 19 Kislev, when they would divide the entire Gemara into sections to be studied that year.

I remember one 19 Kislev farbrengen in his home, when I took a little too much l'chaim. My uncle took me by the arm to my home, which was a long walk. When my father saw me, he asked me if I knew which world I was in, and I answered, "*Shema Yisroel Hashem Elokeinu Hashem echad . . .*"

Another fond memory was that, after 1915, when the Rebbe Rashab moved from Lubavitch to Rostov and it became difficult for the Chassidim in Dokshitz to see the Rebbe (at the time, Dokshitz was in Poland), Oreh's son Beines would go back and forth across the borders, risking his life for a chance to be in the Rebbe's presence.

More about the duo Reb Yekusiel and Reb Aaron can be found in the Rebbe Rayatz's talks Likutei Diburim, vol. 1, p. 91b; ibid., p. 118b; Sefer Hasichos Kayitz 5700, p. 29; Sefer Hasichos Kayitz 5707, p. 113; Sefer Hasichos Kayitz 5708, p. 247; and Sefer Hasichos Kayitz 5710, pp. 351 and 374.

Reb Yisroel Ber

My maternal grandfather, Reb Yisroel Ber Rubin, was born and raised in Zembin, where his close friend was Reb Avraham Landa, the city's rabbi. Later, when Grandfather married a second time, he moved to Velizh, his new wife's hometown, where he became known as Reb Yisroel Ber "Velizher."

Grandfather was a Chassidic scholar and wrote a commentary on the *Tanya*. I have never seen it, however, because after his passing, when his youngest daughter, my aunt, became of marriageable age, my uncle sold the work to the Chassidim in the city to pay for her wedding. What happened to the manuscript afterward, I do not know.

Later in life Grandfather became a book merchant and would go from house to house with his stock of books.

*The Previous Rebbe once told (*Likutei Diburim *[English translation], vol. 3, p. 200) how Reb Yisroel Ber went into yechidus with the Rebbe Maharash:*

> Among the prominent Chassidim who had formed a close bond with my grandfather was Reb Yisrael Dovber, one of the most proficient teachers in Velizh. An intelligent man, he had a keen understanding both of the revealed levels of the Torah and of Chassidus, and engaged earnestly in the service of davening. As a young man he had twice visited my great-grandfather, the Tzemach Tzedek.
>
> From Rosh Hashanah of the year 1866 he visited my grandfather in Lubavitch every year, and was admitted to a private audience on each occasion. In 1902, he told me that at one such an audience, in 1878, he had handed the Rebbe a note that said that though he toiled until he thoroughly grasped a concept in Chassidus, he did so without relish.
>
> My grandfather responded: "Toil is no match for an insensitive mind; what you need is melody in your prayers."
>
> R. Yisrael Dovber recalled, "Your grandfather's reply made me quite despondent. When a man has been toiling away at his service for twelve years, intellectual insensitivity is no great ornament. So, thoroughly downhearted, after the

repetition of the Chassidic discourses of Rosh Hashanah, I told the present Rebbe, your father, of my audience.

The Rebbe Rashab replied, "If one's mind is not exhilarated by a concept, then no matter how thoroughly comprehensible that concept may be, this indicates that it was not truly grasped and that the absence of exhilaration is due to one's intellectual insensitivity."

He then further explained the meaning of "What you need is melody in your prayers," and said that this teaching constituted the individualized help that a Rebbe gives his Chassid.

Reb Yisrael Dovber concluded his reminiscence, "That's exactly what happened. I became a new man. After praying, I would experience an intense yearning to study and master some concept in Chassidus; then, having studied and mastered that concept, I would feel a powerful desire to daven."

A Marriage Made in Lubavitch

Reb Yisroel Ber and Reb Yekusiel, my two grandfathers, met in Lubavitch. Though both were devoted Chassidim, they could not have been more outwardly dissimilar. Reb Yisroel Ber dressed well, like an aristocrat, while Reb Yekusiel was not focused on his appearance.

During their conversation, they realized that one of them had a daughter of marriageable age (Chana Devorah) and the other a son (Yosef), both of whom needed to get married. Then and there, they decided that it was a good shidduch, and after receiving the blessings of the Rebbe Maharash, they finalized plans for the marriage. My parents did not meet each other until the chuppah, as was common in those times.

In letters, Reb Yisroel Ber referred to Reb Yekusiel as "my stu-

Lubavitch, 1994.

dent in Chassidus and my teacher in Gemara [nigleh]," because Reb Yekusiel was a rosh yeshiva and would give shiurim. Indeed, even in his old age, though he would sometimes fall asleep in the middle of a class, he continued his teaching schedule.

Rolling Eyes

Until I was eighteen, I studied with my grandfather Reb Yekusiel in the Chabad beis midrash in Dokshitz. These are some of the memories etched in my mind from that time:

When he would lie down on a bench to rest in the beis midrash, Grandfather would look into the Mitteler Rebbe's *Biurei Zohar*. [He did not appear to be reading,] because his eyes were rolling from side to side. I didn't understand the meaning of this, but, as our sages say (Avodah Zarah 5b), "A student does not understand the reasoning of his teacher until the age of forty."

The Smoke

Grandfather was able-bodied and physically strong and could tolerate a lot. He would sleep in the beis midrash, and when all of the wood finished burning, it happened that he closed the oven door to retain the heat. This trapped the smoke inside as well, and when people arrived in the morning to daven, they coughed and choked on the smoke that had filled the room overnight. But Grandfather didn't seem to be bothered by it.

Lubavitch Memories

Grandfather took me to Lubavitch several times. We would first go to the home where he always stayed on his visits. The man of the house was known as the *Kohen Gadol*. On one of the days of Chol Hamoed Sukkos, there was a farbrengen at the home, which a lot of Chassidim attended. Afterward, everyone went to the Rebbe's farbrengen.

Grandfather and I missed the farbrengen, but we made it in time to see the Rebbe [Rashab], who was sitting in the center of the room. Besides for the Rebbe's table, all of the tables and benches had been broken by people standing on them. Even the bimah was broken in several places, and had to be held up by the Chassidim.

At one point, the Rebbe turned to my brother-in-law Reb Mendel Futerfas, who was from Dvinsky, and said, "Young man from Dvinsk, please hold up the table." In another corner, Reb Michoel Dvorkin was playing a violin. I am not sure which song he was playing.

The mud that we trudged through on our way home that night could not obscure the light that encompassed us after the farbrengen.

These memories left a deep and eternal impression.

Father and the Maggid

I want to end with memories of my father, of blessed memory. Yosef, "Yoshke Kushes [the son of Kushe]," was a merchant of flour and other food basics. He had a pleasant voice and at farbrengens

Mendel and Hinda with their children and grandchildren in Paris, circa 1946. Sitting (from left): Zalman, Mendel, Hinda, Chana Gorovitz, Yisroel Kugel, Yossel Kugel, Mirel. Standing: Izza Kugel, Dovid, Soreh, Dusia Rivkin, Mordechai Rivkin, Rochel Paltiel, Tzila, Mirel Kugel, and Sholom. On the floor: Osseh and Marik.

was often asked to sing. "Reb Yosef, please sing a nigun."

During my childhood, there were *maggidim* (preachers) who would go from town to town to preach (a mixture of admonishment and the ethical teachings of *Mussar*). In our town, there was one shul of *misnagdim*, where the maggidim would go to give their talks. We once received a report about a maggid in town who spoke harshly against Chassidim and Chassidus, as we would say, quoting from Tehillim (59:7), "They howl like the dog and circle the city." In other words, they howl about Chassidus and Chassidim, rather than circling collecting funds for their institutions.

One Shabbos afternoon, my father was walking to shul to learn, and he met a maggid on the way to give his lecture. The maggid greeted him with a *"Gut Shabbos,"* to which my father responded with some sharp words.

During his talk, the maggid described how one of the Chassidim in the town had spoken disrespectfully to him in response to his greeting. "We have to find out who this person is."

It did not take the misnagdim in the town long to discover that it was my father. In revenge, they reported to the local authorities that he had not enlisted properly in the army. My father went to the Rebbe Rashab and asked what to do. The Rebbe told him that he should not be scared. "Hashem will help you and all will be well."

In the end, nothing happened.

THE WOMEN
Brief Sketches

Hinda Deitsch

Mendel's wife, Hinda, was the daughter of Avrohom Yitzchok and Rochel Leah Shagalovitch. Rochel Leah was the daughter of Reb Yosef Kugel, who was the brother of the famed mashpia Reb Chanoch Hendel, who is often mentioned in the talks of the Previous Rebbe.

Rochel Leah was known as a righteous and pious woman and was a friend of Rebbetzin Shterna Sarah, the wife of the Rebbe Rashab.

Hinda's sister Maryasha Badana married Reb Menachem Mendel Futerfas, and they had four children: Chanoch Hendel (Lieberman), who was a known Chassidic artist; Brocho Serebryanski, wife of Rabbi Zalman Serebryanski, a founder and pillar of the Chabad-Lubavitch community and its institutions in Australia;

Reb Mendel Futerfas (left) with members of the Deitsch family. Sitting (left to right) Rabbi Gershon Schusterman and Zalman. Standing second from the right is Avrohom Moshe.

Esther Golda Shemtov, wife of Rabbi Bentzion Shemtov, shliach of the Previous Rebbe to London; and Rabbi Menachem Mendel, a famed Chassid who later in life was the mashpia of the yeshiva in Kfar Chabad, Israel. Reb Mendel was named after his father, who passed away from typhus before Reb Mendel was born.

During a visit to Lubavitch, Rochel Leah asked Rebbetzin Shterna Sarah if she could please bring her young grandson, Mendel Futerfas, who was eight at the time, into yechidus with the Rebbe Rashab.

The Rebbetzin agreed, and after yom tov she took him to the Rebbe, saying, "He is named after his father, and he is the grandson of Rochel Leah. Please accept him into yechidus and give him a blessing."

The Rebbe accepted him into yechidus and blessed him. "You should be a G-d-fearing Jew with long years." Reb Mendel passed away in 5755 (1995), at the age of eighty-seven.

AVROHOM MOSHE DEITSCH

Mirel, as a teenager, with her school friends.

Mirel Deitsch

Zalman's mother, Mirel, was the daughter of Menachem Mendel (the son of Zalman Yudah and Tzipah Sarah Rubin) and Alta Shula (the daughter of Yosef and Chana Devorah Deitsch).

Alta Shula was the granddaughter of Reb Yisroel Ber of Velizher from her mother's side, and from her father's side, the granddaughter of Reb Yekusiel of Dokshitz.

During World War II, Mirel's mother, Alta Shula, passed away from an illness when she was young. Her father and brother, Yisroel Ber, passed away from hunger during the Siege of Leningrad.

EPITOME OF THE DEITSCH FAMILY

By Rabbi Yehoshuah Dubrawsky

The Mishnah states (Peah 7:1) in regard to the law that after one has finished sheaving and forgets something in the field that it goes to the poor. This law is known as *shikchah*:

An olive tree that is well-known from a field . . . is not subject to the laws of shikchah.

Regarding what did they say this?

Regarding an olive tree which is known for its name, for its produce, or for its place.

What does "for its name" mean? That it was *shifchuni* ["A tree that gives fruit which the oil pours forth from it"] or *bayashuni* ["A tree that gives such good fruit that it puts the other trees to shame"].

What does "for its produce" mean? That it produces a

great amount of fruit.

What does "for its place" mean? That it stands near a wine press or near a hole [in a fence].

Reb Mendel Deitsch is like the tree laden with fruit, on which the verse states, "Man is like a tree." With his *name* alone, he drew from those broken souls who would flock to him the praise of being pure olive oil to feed and soothe them.

This "tree" excelled in three things. In its *actions*—rich, good deeds; in its *place*, for he stood ready with an open heart and hand during the time when there was a "hole," when people were homeless, wandering from place to place. Thirdly, indeed, there is no *forgetting*!

Dark ruins stand before me, the city of Samarkand during those terrible days of the early 1940s. It was a time of hunger and pain that landed like the black wings of a bird of prey, which darkened the sun's light and dimmed the internal spark of life. Human skeletons wandered the streets with looks of starvation and agony. Relatives fought over a bread crumb. Siblings cut a small sliver of bread into three. Oy, could the bread have been any smaller?

The sick wandered through the streets and alleyways with faces of hopelessness, cooling their high fever with the dirty water of the pond. They searched for a corner to place their worn-out bodies, crouching in low crevices, like small animals. People were frightened for their small store of possessions. Terrified of the hunger that was always lurking, they feared the next day.

Like diamonds, here and there, with their Jewish compassion, there were those who willingly divided their bread into three and four to share. Some even opened their homes to those who had typhus and other illnesses. However . . . it is better to be silent.

But there was one lighthouse that rose above all the others. I did not know Reb Mendel in the good times. Only from afar did I hear of his good and glorious name and his blessed deeds. I got to know him in this *place*—in the lowest situation of pain and human suffering—when his greatness, his excellence, was expressed.

There was no sign on the Deitsch home. He did not organize a rescue mission, but the hungry knew the way. Years later, he would say, "I arrived in Samarkand with several gold coins, and I decided to save Jews from hunger."

Reb Mendel did not look or speak down to us. He stood with us and gave us a feeling of equality and brotherly love. There was one person who, despite the great hunger, could not bring himself to accept handouts. Reb Mendel turned to him with a radiant smile, "Come! What are you waiting for?"

There was almost nothing that revealed the "owner" of the home, and that we were hungry guests. Reb Mendel was the soul of humility, both in the way he walked the streets and in the way he sat at his table.

As strange as it sounds, I do not remember him ever being alone. Whether he was holding his tallis and tefillin, a large sefer, or a sack of potatoes on his shoulder, there was always someone with him.

He carried the potatoes through the muddy alleys the same way he carried his tefillin to shul, with simplicity and fear of G-d. His entire being was occupied in doing good for another Jew. "What value does a gold coin have," Reb Mendel would say, "compared to sustenance for one hungry soul?"

Our sages say (Mishnah, Sanhedrin 5:4), "Saving one soul is like saving an entire world." In that case, how many complete worlds did Reb Mendel save? One more Jew at his table, one more G-dly soul, another world. He did not measure characters. "The main thing is that there should be one more Jew near the pot of food," said Mendel. A Polish Torah scholar, a porter from Krakow, a Lithuanian yeshiva student, a barefoot child, a shochet from some Russian town . . . they all had a place at the Deitsch table.

I never saw the pot that Mendel's life partner, Hinda, cooked the food in, but it must have been very large. When and how did they prepare such a large amount? There is no place for questions. Mendel disliked questions.

Today we cannot have any grasp of what those hot kneidlach meant for the shriveled mouths and throats. But even more important was the warmth, the homey feeling that accompanied every spoonful of soup, the simple way Reb Mendel sat with everyone around the table.

Just as important as the giving, our sages make clear, is the way tzedakah is given. Reb Mendel made people feel good. With his smile, the look in his eyes, a few rubles pushed into an empty pocket, a gentle hand placed on a hunched shoulder, he opened people's hearts.

The Child

A young child had arrived in Samarkand from Poland by himself and sought refuge in the attic of someone's home. He looked like a skeleton from hunger and had lost his spirit and desire to live. Around him was quiet; no one seemed to know he existed.

The dark nights brought him frightening dreams. His strength was slowly leaving him, melting his very being away. His feet could not hold his failing body.

Somehow Mendel heard his groans. He came just in time, with a bag of food. He refused to leave until the boy ate something. "Nu, nu, don't be foolish. You are not a baby. You know how to put in your mouth a piece of bread with butter on it."

If the child could not eat bread and butter, Mendel brought rice cooked in butter. If he could not eat that, he would bring cheese and sour cream, or something else he thought the child would eat.

The child once told me, "It seemed to me that Reb Mendel was fighting the angel of death, when he found me in this forsaken place."

Soon, the child was able to leave the attic and head to the Deitsch home. It was seldom that Reb Mendel openly showed emotion, but when he saw the boy for the first time around the table, tears rolled down his cheeks. He quickly wiped them away.

The Neighbors

The Deitsches' courtyard was next to a lake. The locals sat on the other side of the lake, giving dirty looks to Reb Mendel and anyone else emerging from the house. But with time, their harsh stares became soft, and their faces emanated warmth. They came to accept the Deitsches' arrival.

I cannot forget the words of one elderly man, who pointed to the Deitsch courtyard, "Only G-d could send to our world such angels in the form of men."

At times, it seemed as if the deep lake and old trees that surrounded it were themselves singing a song of praise to the Deitsch family.

A Different Kind of Teacher

Reb Mendel lived a different type of life. He was not sunk in materialism and had a clear understanding of this world and the next. His shining eyes were capable of seeing through the veil of concealment that people wrapped around themselves.

When he taught *Ein Yaakov*, the sparkle in his eyes made the characters from the Mishnah and Gemara brighter. His feeling of closeness to his listeners brought those righteous people closer to them as well.

Is this all a eulogy? Not at all. Reb Mendel would never have allowed himself to be eulogized. He would have dismissed the idea with a wave of his hand. "What nonsense!"

This is only a little glimpse of his amazing life. It is my hope that my children, and the children of others, should know that their parents received much material and spiritual sustenance in Reb Mendel's courtyard. He is a man who will not be forgotten.

Our sages say (Sanhedrin 111a), "It is a pity for those who are gone and are *lo mishtakchin!*" The words *lo mishtakchin* are usually translated as "no longer to be found." I would like to offer an alternative translation, that *mishtakchin* here be read as "forgotten."

It is a great pain for us, those who are gone but will never be forgotten.

Freely adapted into English from the Yiddishe Heim, *Adar II 5727.*

GLOSSARY

alav hashalom (*pl.* ***aleihem hashalom***). "Peace onto him" (Heb). An honorific, used after the name, for the deceased.

abi gezunt. "As long as one is healthy" (Yid).

Achron shel Pesach. The last day of Passover (Heb). It is known to have a special connection with Moshiach* and is marked with a Moshiach *seuda** (feast) during the last hours of the holiday.

aliyah. "Ascent" (Heb). In a prayer service, the term describes the honor of being called up to the reading table to make a blessing on the Torah* scroll before it is read.

anash. An acronym for *anshei shlomeinu*, "people of our brotherhood" (Heb). It refers to the followers of a specific philosophy or Chassidic group. Here, Chabad* Chassidim.

avodah. "Service" or "work" (Heb). Here, divine service. See also *daven.**

azoi. Like this (Yid).

baal peh. "By heart" (Heb). Memorization is considered an especially praiseworthy form of Torah* study.

baal teshuvah. "Master of return" (Heb). Here, a person who chooses Jewish observance, as opposed to being born in an observant family.

bochur (*pl.* ***bochurim***). "Young man" (Heb). Yeshiva* students over the age of bar mitzvah.*

bar mitzvah. "Son of the commandment" (Heb). At the age of thirteen, a boy passes into adulthood and becomes fully obligated in Jewish observance. The event is usually marked by honoring the boy during Shabbat services, and with a celebration afterward.

Baruch Hashem. "Blessed is G-d" (Heb).

Beis Hamikdash. The Holy Temple in Jerusalem, built and destroyed twice. The first Temple was completed in 2935/827 BCE, the second in 3412/349 BCE. The third, and last, will be built with the coming of Moshiach.*

beis midrash. Study hall (Heb).

bentch (*present and noun: bentching*; *past: bentched*). "To bless" (Yid). Usually the recitation of Grace after Meals.

berachah. Blessing (Heb). The recitation of blessings on every food and beverage, as well as a host of other daily experiences, is an important part of Jewish life. Here, the term also refers to blessings bestowed by a righteous person.

besimchah. With joy (Heb).

bimah. "Platform" (Heb). The elevated table in a synagogue where the Torah* is read.

bitachon. Trust in G-d (Heb).

bris (*pl. brisin*). "Covenant" (Heb). The ritual circumcision of a Jewish boy, performed at eight days old.

Chabad. An acronym for the Hebrew words *chochmah, binah,* and *daas* (wisdom, understanding, and knowledge). Chabad is a branch of the Chassidic movement that takes an intellectual approach to the service of G-d. In the second half of the twentieth century, Chabad became known for its dedication to bolstering Jewish observance. See also Lubavitch.*

chachmas chitzoiniyos. "External wisdom" (Heb). General studies, as opposed to Torah.*

chametz. "Leaven" (Heb). Any food made of wheat, barley, oats, spelt, or rye that has come into contact with water and been allowed to ferment for more than eighteen minutes. Jews are forbidden to consume, or even own, *chametz* on Passover.

Chanukah. The eight-day holiday celebrating the rededication of the Holy Temple in Jerusalem in the second century BCE, observed by kindling an additional light on a nine-branched candelabra (menorah*) each night.

chassan. Groom (Heb).

Chassid (*pl. Chassidim*). A member of the Chassidic movement with allegiance to a rebbe,* Chassidic leader, or to a particular Chassidic philosophy.

Chassidism (*Yid. Chassidishkeit*); **Chassidus.** From the Hebrew word *chassid* (pious), the Chassidic movement was founded in the eighteenth century by Rabbi Israel ben Eliezer, known as the Baal Shem Tov. Chassidic teachings (*Chassidus*) use the mystical writings of the Kabbalah to illuminate the deeper significance of Jewish prayer and observance. A Chassid serves G-d with love and joy, recognizing the role of divine providence in every aspect of his or her life.

Chassidishe. Chassidic (Yid). A *Chassidishe* lifestyle is characterized by an uncompromising adherence to Chassidic customs and nuances.

chazarah. "Repetition" (Heb). Among Chabad* Chassidim,* reviewing a talk or discourse of a rebbe.*

chazzan. Cantor (Heb). One who leads prayer services in synagogue.

cheder. "Room" (Heb). Originally a one-room school where Jewish boys were taught Hebrew and religious studies. Today it is used to describe religious primary schools.

chinuch. "Education" (Heb). Jewish education.

Chitas. An acronym for Chumash (the Pentateuch), Tehillim* (Psalms), and *Tanya.* Chabad* Chassidim* (and many others) study a portion of each work daily, according to a specific schedule.

Chol Hamoed. The intermediate days of Passover and Sukkos* when, with some exceptions, regular weekday activities are permitted.

chozrim (*s. chozer*). A select group of individuals who were tasked with memorizing the Rebbe's* talks on Shabbos* and festivals, and then reviewing them afterward so that they could be recorded.

Chumash. The Five Books of Moses, the Pentateuch.

chuppah. "Canopy" (Heb). The marriage ceremony, performed under a canopy. The custom of many, including Chabad,* is to hold the *chuppah* under the open sky.

daven (*present:* ***davening***). The act of praying (Yid). Chabad* tradition puts great emphasis on ***davening b'avodah***, serving G-d through prayer, which includes contemplating G-d's greatness, how He recreates the world from nothing every moment and controls even the most minor events. Prayer with deep concentration is often accompanied by a *nigun.**

dayanus. From the word *dayan* "judge" (Heb). The course of study required to become a rabbinic judge.

Dovid Hamelech. King David.

dvar Torah. "A word of Torah" (Heb). A Torah* idea shared with others, often at the Shabbos* or *yom tov** table.

emunah. Faith in G-d (Heb).

Eretz Yisroel. The Land of Israel (Heb).

farbrengen. "Spending time [together]" (Yid). A formal or informal assembly where Chassidic teachings and stories are shared and *nigunim** are sung. Intended to renew the Chassid's* fervor for divine service, farbrengens are an integral part of Chassidic life. The Chabad* Rebbes* used farbrengens to share words of inspiration, Torah* ideas, and original Chassidic discourses. **Farbreng:** To take part in or lead a farbrengen.

freilech. Joyous (Yid).

gabai. A synagogue's beadle or sexton (Heb).

galus. Exile (Heb). Usually refers to the historic exile of the Jews from the Land of Israel, after the destruction of the Holy Temple. See also Beis ̦Hamikdash.*

gartel. A sash or cord worn around the waist by Chassidic men and other religious Jews during prayer services, marking a symbolic separation between the higher and lower (less spiritual) parts of the body.

gemach. An acronym for the Hebrew *gemilas chassidim* (acts of kindness), it usually refers to a free loan society.

Gemara. From the Aramaic word "to study," the commentary and discussion of the sages which, together with the Mishnah* (oral laws), constitute the Talmud. Completed in the year 475 CE, the Gemara is the basis for the Code of Jewish Law, and its study, almost always accompanied by lively debate, is the foundation of Jewish education. In common usage, "Talmud" and "Gemara" are used interchangeably.

Geulah. "Redemption" (Heb). Here, the final Redemption with the coming of Moshiach.*

gomel. "The one who grants" (Heb). The blessing, recited publicly, by a person who has survived a dangerous situation, such as a flight overseas or surgery.

gut Shabbos. "Good Sabbath" (Yid). The traditional salutation for the Sabbath.

hachnosas orchim. "Welcoming guests" (Heb). The biblical commandment to welcome guests into one's home.

Haftorah. The portion of the prophets recited following the weekly Torah* reading in synagogue.

halachah. "The way" (Heb). Jewish law, as codified in the Shulchan Aruch, the Code of Jewish Law. **Halachos:** individual laws.

Hashem. "The Name" (Heb). An informal way of referring to G-d without using the divine name in vain.

Havdalah. "Separation" (Heb). The prayer and ceremony marking the end of the Sabbath and/or yom tov.*

hiskashrus. "Connection" (Heb). The relationship and spiritual bond between a Chassid* and his rebbe.*

Kaddish. "Holy" (Heb). A prayer recited by the cantor at various points during the prayer service. It is also recited by mourners during the funeral and during prayer services for the first eleven months after the passing of an immediate relative, and on a yahrtzeit.*

kallah. Bride (Heb).

kein ayin hara. "No evil eye" (Yid). The Yiddish expression used after discussing something good, especially concerning children.

Kiddush. "Sanctification" (Heb). When capitalized, the term refers to the prayer to sanctify the day, recited before the Shabbos* or yom tov* meal, over a cup of wine. Informally, a kiddush is the spread of refreshments served in synagogue following the Shabbos morning prayer service.

Kiddush Hachodesh. "Sanctification of the month" (Heb). The complicated laws regarding when the new Jewish month begins.

Kinus Hashluchim (Heb). The annual gathering of Chabad-Lubavitch* emissaries at Lubavitch Headquarters in the Crown Heights neighborhood of Brooklyn, New York.

Kohen Gadol. High Priest (Heb). A descendant of Aaron, brother of Moses, the Kohen Gadol led services and performed special sacrifices in the Holy Temple in Jerusalem.

Kol Nidrei. "All the Oaths" (Heb). The pivotal prayer recited at the onset of the Yom Kippur services, it releases a person from all the resolutions and promises they made during the past year.

kollel (Heb). An advanced Torah* academy for married men.

kos shel berachah. "Cup of blessing" (Heb). After a holiday, Chassidim* would line up to receive a little wine from the cup the Rebbe* had used for Havdalah,* and with it, a blessing.

Krias Shema al Hamitah (Heb). The recitation of the Shema prayer, a declaration of faith in the unity of G-d, and other select prayers, before retiring for the night.

l'chaim. "To life" (Heb). The traditional Jewish toast. At a *farbrengen,** participants toast each other, offering blessings for material and spiritual abundance. Also, a small glass of wine or liquor used to make a toast.

lekach. Honey cake (Yid). Honey cake distributed by the Rebbe on the eve of Yom Kippur, with wishes for a sweet year. It is customary to ask for a piece in the hope that it will be the only thing one needs to ask for that year.

likut. "Collection" (Heb). A collection of the Rebbe's* talks edited by the Rebbe and published weekly as a pamphlet.

Lubavitch; Lubavitcher. Literally "the town of love," Lubavitch is the name for the Russian village where the Chabad movement was based for over a century. The movement, its followers, and leaders became known as "Lubavitch" or "Lubavitchers." See also Chabad.*

ma'aver* the *sedra. "Review the weekly portion" (Heb). The practice of reciting the weekly Torah* portion, together with its Aramaic translation, twice on Friday.

maamar (*pl.* ***maamarim***). "Utterance" (Heb). A formal discourse of Chassidic philosophy delivered by a Chabad* rebbe.*

maariv. The evening prayer service.

maggid (*pl.* ***maggidim***). A preacher (Heb).

malach. Angel (Heb).

mashke. "Liquid" (Heb). An alcoholic beverage.

mashpia. "Mentor" (Heb). A spiritual mentor, either in a yeshiva* or in civilian life. The Rebbe* encouraged all his followers to choose a *mashpia.*

matzah. Unleavened, cracker-like bread eaten during Passover. It commemorates the Exodus from Egypt, when the Jews fled in such haste that they did not have time to let their bread rise.

matzeiva. Tombstone (Heb).

mefarshim. Commentaries (Heb).

Megillah. "Scroll" (Heb). Here, the *Scroll of Esther,* read on the holiday of Purim.

Melave Malka. "Escorting the queen" (Heb). The Saturday-night meal to bid farewell to the Sabbath Queen.

menachem avel. The mitzvah to comfort a mourner (Heb).

menorah. The eight-branched candelabra lit on every night of Chanukah* in commemoration of the miracle that took place during the rededication of the Holy Temple in the second century BCE, when a small amount of oil, enough for one night, burned for eight days.

mesiras nefesh. "Self-sacrifice" (Heb). Giving up personal interests, even one's life, for observance.

mezuzah (Heb). The parchment scroll affixed on the doorposts of the rooms in a Jewish home or business, containing portions of the Shema.

mikvah (Heb). A ritual bath built according to the detailed specifications of Jewish law. Married women are obligated to immerse in a mikvah every month, but men may also use it to improve their spiritual state.

minchah. The afternoon prayer, said before sunset. Minchah is an important service, since at times it requires one to interrupt the day's business to pray, highlighting one's devotion to G-d.

minyan. "The count" (Heb). The quorum of ten men needed for communal prayer service.

Mishnah (pl. Mishnayos). The first written compilation of the oral law, authored by Rabbi Yehudah Hanasi (c. 200 CE). It is comprised of the germinal statements of law, later elucidated by the Gemara*; also a single statement of law from this work.

misnagdim. "The opponents" (Heb). Referring to Jews who opposed the Chassidic movement.

mivtzoim. The mitzvah campaigns instituted by the Rebbe; also used informally for the practice of promoting those campaigns by approaching Jews individually on the street or in the workplace.

mohel. The trained individual who performs ritual circumcisions.

Moshiach. "The anointed one" (Heb). The one who will lead the Jewish nation to the Redemption and usher in a new age when "the Earth shall be full of knowledge of the L-rd, as the waters cover the sea" (Isaiah 11:9). Belief in the coming of Moshiach is one of the core principles of Jewish faith.

Motzei Shabbos. After dark on Saturday night, when the Sabbath is over.

mugah. "Edited" (Heb). Here, transcribed talks of the Rebbe,* edited by the Rebbe himself.

nachas; nachas ruach. Satisfaction and pleasure derived from the good deeds of those on whom one has had an influence, particularly children.

Neilah. "The closing" (Heb). The fifth prayer service, recited before the conclusion of Yom Kippur, just before the gates of Heaven "close."

neshamah. Soul (Heb).

nigleh. "Revealed" (Heb). The non-mystical part of Torah,* especially the Talmud and Jewish law.

nigun (pl. nigunim). A Chassidic melody, often wordless and repeated several times, intended to express and stir the soul.

ohel. "Tent" (Heb). The resting place of a righteous person. Here, "the Ohel" is the resting place of the sixth and seventh Chabad* rebbes* in Queens, New York.

pan. An acronym for *pidyon*

nefesh, "redemption of the soul" (Heb). A letter, usually containing a request for blessings, given to a rebbe* or torn and placed at his gravesite.

panim chadashos. "New face" (Heb). It is a requirement to invite a new face—someone who did not attend the wedding—to every *sheva berachos** so that the seven blessings may be recited with new joy.

parsha. "Portion" (Heb). The portion read from the Torah* scroll in synagogue during the week and on Shabbos.* The Torah is divided into fifty-four portions and is completed once a year.

passuk (Heb). A biblical verse.

Pegisha. "Encounter" (Heb). Weekend retreats organized by the Lubavitch Youth Organization to introduce Jews to Jewish observance and the Chassidic community, held in the Crown Heights neighborhood in Brooklyn, New York.

pidyon haben. "Redemption of the son" (Heb). Jewish law requires the redemption of a first-born son by giving five silver coins to a *kohen* (a member of the priestly family). The occasion is celebrated with a festive meal.

pilpul. An in-depth analytical investigation of a Torah* topic (Heb).

platz. Place (Yid).

pushka. "Container" (Heb). A charity box.

rebbe. "Teacher" (Heb). The term also refers to a Chassidic leader. In this book, "the Rebbe" is the seventh Lubavitcher Rebbe, Rabbi Menachem Mendel Schneerson (1902–1994).

rosh yeshiva. The dean of a yeshiva.*

seder. "Order" (Heb). The ritual service performed on the first two nights of Passover. It includes the *mitzvot* of eating matzah* and bitter herbs and drinking four cups of wine.

sefer (*pl.* ***seforim***). A Torah* book (Heb).

semichah. "To lean on" (Heb). Rabbinical ordination.

seuda (Heb). A Shabbos* or *yom tov** meal.

Shabbos. The Jewish Sabbath, which commemorates the completion of the Six Days of Creation and G-d's resting on the seventh day. It is observed each week from sunset on Friday until Saturday night with festive meals and special prayer services. Weekday activities such as driving, writing, and cooking are prohibited on Shabbos.

Shabbos Mevorchim. "Shabbos When We Bless" (Heb). The Sabbath before the start of a new Hebrew month, when *Birchas Hachodesh* (blessing for the new month) is recited. Chabad* custom is to recite the entire book of Psalms before morning services on that day.

shadchanus. "Matchmaking" (Heb). Here, the payment given to a matchmaker.

shalom. Peace (Heb). A salutation for greeting or parting.

Shavuos. "Weeks" (Heb). The holiday marking the Giving of the Torah.* It is customary to stay awake on the first night of Shavuos to study Torah.

Shemini Atzeres. The seventh and eighth days of Sukkos* are considered a separate holiday, celebrated with great joy. In the Diaspora, the eighth day is Simchas Torah.*

sheva berachos. The seven blessings recited under the wedding canopy and meals during the week of festivities following the wedding.

sheyichyu. "They should live" (Heb). An honorific used after the name of someone who is alive. Contrast with *alav hashalom.* *

shidduch (Heb). An arranged match, usually made by a matchmaker.

shiur (*pl.* **shiurim**) (Heb). A Torah* study class.

shiva. The seven-day mourning period observed after the passing of a close relative.

shliach (*pl.* **shluchim**); **shlichus.** "Emissary" (Heb). Here, a Chabad* representative who becomes an emissary by moving to a community in order to strengthen Jewish observance or assist an established Chabad House. The representatives' mission is their shlichus.

shloshim. "Thirty" (Heb). The thirty-day mourning period after the passing of a close relative.

shmates. Rags (Yid). Here, the textile industry.

shochet. A person trained to ritually slaughter animals according to Jewish law.

shofar. A hollowed-out ram's horn sounded on Rosh Hashanah, at the close of Yom Kippur, and every day during the month of Elul.

shtiebel. "Small house" (Yid). A small synagogue, usually Chassidic.

shul. Synagogue (Yid).

sichah (pl. **sichos**). A talk (Heb). Here, a talk given by the Rebbe.*

siddur (pl. **siddurim**). Prayer book (Heb).

simchah (pl. **simchos**). Joyous occasions (Heb).

Simchas Torah. "Rejoicing of the Torah" (Heb). The holiday that celebrates the completion of the yearly Torah* reading cycle (see also parsha*). In the Diaspora, Simchas Torah is observed on the second day of Shemini Atzeres.*

sukkah. A small hut erected outdoors, roofed with branches. It commemorates the clouds that protected the Jews as they traveled through the desert from Egypt to the Land of Israel. During the holiday of Sukkos,* all meals and regular activities are conducted in the sukkah.

Sukkos. The eight-day festival that follows the High Holy Days of Rosh Hashanah and Yom Kippur, celebrated by dwelling in a sukkah* and the mitzvah of the Four Kinds.

tafkid. One's life mission (Heb).

tahalucha. "March" (Heb). The Rebbe* instituted the tradition for Chabad* Chassidim* to walk (often long distances) to bring cheer to other congregations on the holidays of Passover and Shavuos.*

tallis. Prayer shawl (Heb).

Tanya. The fundamental text of Chabad* Chassidism, written by the movement's founder, Rabbi Shneur Zalman of Liadi, known as the Alter Rebbe.

Tefilas Haderech. The prayer for travelers.

tefillin. Black leather boxes containing parchment scrolls worn by Jewish males, beginning two months before their bar mitzvah,* on the arm and the head during weekday morning prayers in fulfillment of the command, "You shall bind them as a sign upon your hand, and they shall be for you a reminder between your eyes" (Deuteronomy 6:8).

Tehillim. The book of Psalms.

teshuvah. "Return" (Heb). Often translated as "repentance," teshuvah includes the review of past misdeeds and the resolution to return to the correct path.

Torah. The Bible (Five Books of Moses); the Torah scroll; used loosely for the general corpus of Jewish teachings.

tzaddik (*pl. tzaddikim*). A righteous person (Heb).

tzedakah. "Righteousness" (Heb). The mitzvah to help others financially (charity) or spiritually.

tzidkeinu. "Our righteous one" (Heb). An honorific used for Moshiach.*

tziyun. "Marker" (Heb). Here, a tombstone.

ufruf. "Call up" (Yid). A groom is called up to bless the Torah* on the Sabbath before his wedding, an occasion traditionally followed by a small celebration.

yahrtzeit. The anniversary of someone's passing (Yid).

yechidus. A private audience with a rebbe.*

yeshiva. "To sit" (Heb). Traditionally, the term referred to a higher academy of Torah* study. Today, any Jewish day school or academy may be called a yeshiva.

Yidden. Jews (Yid).

Yiddishkeit. "Judaism" (Yid). Here, Jewish observance.

yom tov (*pl. yomim tovim*). "Good day" (Heb). A Jewish holiday.

Yud Tes Kislev. Known as the New Year of Chassidism, it celebrates the day that the founder of Chabad,* Rabbi Shneur Zalman of Liadi, known as the Alter Rebbe, was liberated from prison in Czarist Russia in 5559/1798.